Penguin Education

Penguin Modern Economics Texts
General Editor: B. J. McCormick

008385

International Econon
Editor: J. Spraos

The International Monetary System
Efficiency and Practical Alternatives
Herbert G. Grubel

The International Monetary System

Efficiency and Practical Alternatives

Herbert G. Grubel

Penguin Books

Penguin Books Ltd, Harmondsworth,
Middlesex, England
Penguin Books Inc, 7110 Ambassador Road,
Baltimore, Maryland 21207, U.S.A.
Penguin Books Australia Ltd, Ringwood,
Victoria, Australia

First published by Penguin Books Ltd 1969
First published by Penguin Books Inc 1970
Reprinted 1972, 1974

Printed in the United States of America by
Universal Lithographers, Inc.
Set in Linotype Times

Penguin Modern Economics Texts

This volume is one in a series of unit texts designed to reduce the price of knowledge for students of economics in universities and colleges of higher education. The units may be used singly or in combination with other units to form attractive and unusual teaching programmes. The volumes will cover the major teaching areas but they will differ from conventional books in their attempt to chart and explore new directions in economic thinking. The traditional divisions of theory and applied, of positive and normative and of micro and macro will tend to be blurred as authors impose new and arresting ideas on the traditional corpus of economics. Some units will fall into conventional patterns of thought but many will transgress established beliefs.

Penguin Modern Economics Texts are published in units in order to achieve certain objectives. First, a large range of short texts at inexpensive prices gives the teacher flexibility in planning his course and recommending texts for it. Secondly, the pace at which important new work is published requires the project to be adaptable. Our plan allows a unit to be revised or a fresh unit to be added with maximum speed and minimal cost to the reader.

The international range of authorship will, it is hoped, bring out the richness and diversity in economic analysis and thinking.

B.J.McC.

To my wife

Contents

Editorial Foreword 11

Preface 13

Part One **Characteristics of an Efficient World Monetary Order 17**

1 International Monetary Organization in Perspective 19

2 Reserves and Exchange Rate Stability 28

3 Other Determinants of the Demand for Reserves 45

4 The Adequacy of a World Monetary Order and Types of Reform 75

Part Two **The Theory and History of Organizational Prototypes 87**

5 The Gold Standard 89

6 Freely Fluctuating Exchange Rates 107

7 The Gold Exchange Standard 128

8 Centrally Created Reserves 151

References 187

Index 198

Editorial Foreword

This textbook is one of at least six which will attempt to cover between them the main sub-areas of International Economics. Two, including the present one, appear in the initial batch of *Penguin Modern Economics Texts*. The others will follow in fairly quick succession.

International Economics is the oldest branch of Economics viewed as a discipline and the second oldest (after Public Finance) viewed as an area of practical concern for a national economy. The first extant account of England's balance of trade goes back to 1355! It hardly needs saying, however, that it is not for antiquarian reasons that International Economics commands attention at the present time. Any alert citizen knows that some of the most pressing and frequently the most intractable economic problems are international in character.

The subject-matter of this volume has acquired such enormous importance in recent years that it is easy to forget that problems associated with an international monetary system must have existed ever since countries with independent currencies began trading with each other. By concentrating on general principles the author brings out the continuing relevance of many problems, and gives the student a conceptual and analytical framework to help his understanding of the shifting pattern of events.   J.S.

Preface

The first part of this book contains the theoretical model of an efficient world monetary system. The model's distinguishing feature is that it treats the determination of optimum levels of international reserve supplies and the propensity to make exchange rate changes as parts of an interdependent system in which countries also engage in optimizing domestic price and income adjustments, imposition of direct controls on foreign trade and capital flows, tariff variations and surrender of national sovereignty through international co-operation. In an efficient world monetary system all of these tools of adjustment are used to the point where a marginal increase in their use yields equal welfare losses when countries deal with external payments imbalances.

The second part of the book uses the theoretical construct of Part One to analyse the blueprints, histories and shortcomings of the four prototypes of international monetary order, the gold standard, freely floating exchange rates, the gold exchange standard and a system of centrally created reserves.

While I was writing this book international monetary problems repeatedly made front page news. In Autumn 1967 the International Monetary Fund meetings in Rio de Janeiro led to an agreement for fundamental reform, which gives the international monetary authority the right to create fiat money. Shortly thereafter the existing gold exchange standard received a serious jolt when the pound sterling was devalued and was further weakened by speculative gold buying. Efforts to deal with the gold speculation resulted in the March 1968 Washington

Agreements, which established a two-price system for gold, \$35 an ounce for official monetary gold transactions and a freely determined market price for private users.

I have tried to incorporate these developments into the text and to interpret them in the light of the theoretical structure of analysis presented in Part One. However, because of the speed with which developments have been taking place and can be expected to continue to do so in the future these discussions have been kept short.

My students, who have read an earlier version of this book urged me to write a concluding chapter in which I state my own recommendations for reform of the inter-national monetary system. I have not followed their advice because the expression of my own views is hardly worth a chapter and can be undertaken more efficiently in this Preface. My first preference is for a new world monetary order based on freely floating exchange rates. The risks and uncertainties of such a system are worth taking in view of the expected benefits, especially if flexibility is limited to rates between optimum geographic regions whose currency markets are so deep that speculators find it difficult to destabilize the rates.

However, if the world's financial establishment is un-willing to accept a system of freely fluctuating exchange rates, I would cast my vote in favour of a system of centrally created reserves, essentially along the lines agreed upon at the Rio de Janeiro meetings, with the change that total reserves be increased at a steady rate of 3 per cent per year and that this rate can be *changed* only by 85 per cent majority vote.

The merits of these recommendations need not be defended here. In my view, the entire book's analysis of the consequences of alternative forms of organization represents a defence of my specific recommendations.

Since this work is designed to be a textbook I have followed tradition and drawn liberally from the existing stock of knowledge without giving explicit credit to the authors of specific ideas and insights. However, the annotated bibliography serves to indicate the overwhelming degree of my intellectual indebtedness to other authors.

Robert Triffin as my teacher at Yale University awakened my initial interest in the problems of world monetary organization and while I have tried to emancipate myself from his specific ideas, I shall forever remain grateful to him for the help and inspiration he has given me as a student. The three years I spent as a professional colleague of Harry G. Johnson at the University of Chicago have taught me standards of intellectual rigour and logical incisiveness which I have little hope of ever attaining. As teachers, friends and idols, these two men have contributed immeasurably to this book.

Several persons have read earlier versions of the manuscript and the comments of A. Bloomfield, B. Grimm, H. G. Johnson, H. Mayer, J. Spraos, D. Vickers and R. Whittlesey were gratefully received and helped me to clarify the analysis and improve style and exposition. My course in International Finance at the University of Pennsylvania served as a testing ground for much of the book's contents and the students' discussions and comments were useful in the preparation of the final manuscript. I am also grateful to Mrs Pamela Fadner, who typed the manuscript cheerfully and efficiently.

Part One   Characteristics of an Efficient World Monetary Order

1 International Monetary Organization in Perspective

As Adam Smith pointed out a long time ago, given resources of labour and capital are more productive the greater the specialization of human skills and machines. However, such increased physical productivity leads to greater material well-being of man only if the products of specialized production can be exchanged efficiently in the market-place. One necessary ingredient for such an efficient exchange is the existence of money, without which there would only be a cumbersome system of barter. Because money is so important in modern times, governments in all countries have taken on the responsibility for the creation and maintenance of national money supplies.

World productivity and the material well-being of man can also be increased by national specialization in production and the international exchange of output. As in national economies, the existence of an efficient financial system facilitates this exchange. However, in contrast with national economies, the world does not possess a central government with coercive powers which can regulate the supply of money or change financial institutions in the interest of maximizing world welfare. Yet, for the international economy the existence of a well-functioning financial system assuring efficient exchange is as important as it is for national economies. For this reason the problems of international monetary organization deserve to be studied with great care.

Technical Problems and Politics

This book presents outlines of alternative forms of international monetary order, discusses their alleged advantages and disadvantages, and examines the available theoretical and empirical evidence about the probable size and distribution of welfare gains and losses which would arise if any one of them were introduced. The book thus tries to present the kind of information needed by politicians to choose a new world monetary order with the full knowledge of the consequences following from the choice.

It lies in the nature of world monetary reform that each alternative reduces or increases by differing amounts the welfare of certain nations, groups of nations, or interest groups within countries. For this reason, the actual negotiations about the reform have to take place at the political level where through bargaining, a process of making concessions and demands, it is finally agreed to adopt a system that is acceptable to the majority of the countries affected by reform. The following analysis of alternatives is designed to aid this bargaining process by making it clearer what the likely effects of alternative courses of action and hidden consequences are. This kind of analysis is likely to be useful for a long time, and certainly beyond conclusion of the negotiations for reform taking place in the late 1960s because negotiations will always result in a political compromise and there is very little chance that a system adopted at any given time will be satisfactory for a long period in the future. The technical conditions of trade and finance will change as world population, income and specialization grow, thus requiring that the world's payments system deal effectively with different sets of problems. Furthermore, changes in the world's distribution of political and military power will be accompanied by demands for the redistribution of the gains from the monetary order more in line with the new pattern of effective power.

The history of reforms in world monetary organization illustrates how they have been influenced by technical changes and shifts in economic and military power. For example, the gold standard functions well only if, as will be seen in more detail later, individual countries do not engage in independent employment policies. When most of the world's population lived off the land in relative self-sufficiency and cyclical instabilities characteristic of capitalist economies had relatively minor welfare effects, the gold standard worked well. But as countries began to industrialize and populations shifted into urban centres, cyclical fluctuations in employment had increasingly more significant effects on the well-being of the public. Pressures mounted on governments to engage in deliberate counter-cyclical policies. The end of *laissez-faire* in national economies also brought to an end the gold standard's usefulness as the system under which the international monetary affairs of the world were carried on.

The redistribution of economic and military power since the end of the Second World War has led to demands for a reorganization of the world monetary mechanism that had evolved during that period. This mechanism is known as the gold exchange standard, whose salient feature is that the United States and to some extent the United Kingdom are the 'World's Banker'. These countries have reserves of gold which they are willing to exchange on demand for dollar and sterling claims held by foreign governments. Because of this exchangeability and a number of other reasons to be discussed in detail in chapter 7, dollars and sterling are widely held by countries as reserves and are used as means of payments in private and intergovernmental transactions. These dollar and sterling claims are thus very much like an international 'money'.

The United States and Britain gain some advantages from issuing this money and from being the World's Banker. Their national prestige is enhanced because the acceptability of the dollar and sterling reflects the world's confidence in the stability and strength of these countries, and, most important, these national obligations require that the United States and the United Kingdom pay only very low interest rates while the countries which acquired them have surrendered real resources or high interest bearing long-term securities in return. As long as the system functions well, the countries serving as the World's Bankers can run continuous deficits and in real terms live better than they could otherwise.

The formation of the European Economic Community in 1958 and the rapid rates of economic development of this era have led to a relative decline in the economic weight of the United States and the United Kingdom. Along with this realignment of power and a new wave of nationalism have come demands from some of the E.E.C. members, most notably France, for a more equitable sharing of the gains from being the World's Banker. They have at one time demanded that the French franc and German mark be used in international settlements and as reserve holdings along with dollars and sterling. At other times France had demanded a return to the gold standard and the abandonment of a system in which there were World Bankers. Any new form of world monetary organization adopted in the future is almost certain to reflect in some measure the essence of these demands, and to satisfy Continental Western Europe's yearning for a role in the world's financial affairs more in line with her new vigour and stature.

Future changes in technology, trade and in the relative strength of countries can only be guessed. There appears to be ahead an intensification of the developing nations' need for capital. Beyond that, there looms the problem of how these countries can service their debts and make repayments on the principal. In the political arena the very populous nations of Asia are certain to become relatively more important than they have been until now. The development of the natural resources of the African and South American continents may raise these areas' demands for a greater voice in international monetary affairs.

As long as there will be these kinds of changes in the world, and it matters little whether they can be forecast accurately or not, the thorough study of the theory and history of world monetary organization will be important for today's students who are tomorrow's monetary technicians, politicians and voters.

Monetary Organization and Other Problems

In this book the focus of the analysis will be on the issues of international monetary organization. However, these issues are related to many other problems besetting some national economies since the end of the Second World War. Foremost, and the most important of those, have been the persistent balance of payments deficits experienced by the United States and the United Kingdom.

Balance of payments difficulties have plagued other Western countries at least once during the post-war period. France, Italy and Canada experienced external payments deficits, while Germany and the Netherlands were embarrassed by persistent large payments surpluses. What differentiated the difficulties of these five major industrial nations from those of the United States and the United Kingdom is the former countries' willingness or ability to use exchange rate adjustments to correct the disequilibria. Some observers may argue that these adjustments did not occur frequently enough or at the most appropriate times, but the fact remains that exchange rate revaluations did take place. The reluctance of the United States and United Kingdom to devalue is importantly related to the current organization of the world monetary system, which makes them reserve currency centres.

As was already explained, these two countries in a certain sense serve as the World's Bankers since their currencies are used as internationally acceptable means of payments. In order to retain the acceptability of the currencies, confidence in their stability and value must be maintained. As will be discussed in chapter 7, an official devaluation tends to destroy this confidence and curtail severely the world's stock of international money, which would reduce the efficiency of international exchange. As a result of this connexion between the United States and the United Kingdom economies and the world's payments system, it has been argued that these two countries have lost the freedom to use devaluation to restore external balance. Instead, these two countries had to use policies which have had very undesirable effects on the welfare of their own citizens as well as those in other countries. The United Kingdom for many years had to engage in periodic drastic measures of internal demand deflation, which caused unemployment and probably resulted in the slow-down of economic growth because continuity in investment planning by industry was made more difficult and because the interest rate had to be kept high for the purpose of attracting foreign financial capital. The reduced demand for foreign products by England in turn made it more difficult for the producers of these exports – some of them underdeveloped nations – to earn the foreign exchange with which to pay for the products they needed to import from industrialized countries in order to further their own development. In 1967 these welfare losses appear to have been judged excessive even in the light of the benefits of Britain's role of World Banker and the pound sterling was devalued. Only after several years will it be possible to judge whether this devaluation has terminated Britain's role as a World Banker. The devaluation's effect on the world's monetary mechanism similarly can be judged only in time and depends significantly on the kinds of institutional innovations adopted in the future. (See chapter 8.)

The United States also suffered unemployment and probably some slow-down in economic growth during the period of about 1958–61 at least in part because balance-of-payments deficits required that monetary policy remained tight while fiscal policy could not be made easier because of political institutional barriers to its use.

When fiscal policy in the form of the 1963–4 tax cuts finally was used to stimulate demand and reduce unemployment, other undesirable methods of reducing the deficit were introduced. There were put into effect 'voluntary' restraints on capital exports by American business, the interest equalization tax was passed, foreign aid was tied to purchases in the United States, military and other government purchases were directed to the home-market, tourist tariff exemptions were reduced, etc. All of these measures represent serious interference with the market's allocative mechanism and the cumulative loss of welfare resulting from these misallocations may be quite large.

A second important problem of the post-war years has been the widening gap in *per capita* incomes between the developed and less developed countries of the world. This problem may become an increasing threat to the political stability of the world, in addition to being a blemish on the record of mankind's development from barbarism to humane civilization.

Humanitarians in nearly all of the industrialized countries have succeeded in establishing programmes of aid to the developing nations. Their task has been made more difficult and probably fewer resources have been transferred because two of the major industrial nations of the West, the United States and the United Kingdom had experienced chronic balance of payments deficits they were unable to rectify efficiently for reasons related to the existing international monetary order, as was just discussed.

A third major set of world problems is due to the existence of tariff and other barriers to the free international movement of goods and services. Some of these tariffs are especially discriminatory against the industrialized countries' importation of those products from underdeveloped countries requiring a high share of labour in value-added, as has been brought out by recent research in the new theory of effective tariff protection. The expected gains in world welfare following from the removal of these barriers to international specialization and trade are very great. The reasons why countries have not tried to obtain these gains by unilateral reductions of barriers and have made only slow progress towards multilateral agreements are complicated, and not all economic in nature. However, it is certain that nations' reluctance to lower restrictions on foreign trade is greater the more difficulty they have to maintain domestic full employment and balance in international payments. The prolonged U.S. and U.K. difficulties in these areas, due in part to the particular form of the world monetary organization, have undoubtedly contributed not only to their slowness in lowering tariffs, but as was argued already, have led to the introduction of more such barriers.

Thus, it can be seen that the major problems facing the international economic community, persistent deficits of the World's Bankers, the growing gap between rich and poor countries, and the existence of barriers to free world trade, are in some important way linked to the operation of the world's payments system. In fact, it is this relationship which has led to the demand for international monetary reform and it will be the reappearance of similar problems in the future which will give rise to the need for still other reforms. However, while there exist these logical connexions between world monetary organization and other national and international economic problems, it would be false to assume that even a new monetary order which is 'ideal' from the point of view of some economists and uncompromised by political deals, would 'solve' the other problems. Income gaps will exist for a long time to come, interest groups within countries will oppose removal of trade barriers and under most organizational systems national payments imbalances will continue to develop periodically. A new international monetary organization will merely reduce the severity of some of these problems.

The following analysis will treat the problem of world monetary organization as logically separate from the other more contemporary problems of the world economy, in spite of the inter-relationships just discussed. This logical separation facilitates the exposition and prevents the theoretical core of the analysis from becoming obsolete in the way discussions of current problems often do.

2 Reserves and Exchange Rate Stability

The present and following two chapters contain a discussion of the nature of international money and a basic theoretical model which shows the inter-relationships between aggregate world demand for international reserves, the flexibility of exchange rates, capital mobility, co-operation among central bankers, cyclical stability of national economies, etc. This theoretical framework serves as a simple scheme for the classification of the reform proposals and prototypes of world monetary order widely discussed by academicians and the public. The model also lends itself to the demonstration of the hidden assumptions, value judgements, gains and benefits each alternative organizational form contains and which are important for a thorough understanding of their merits and weaknesses.

The Nature of International Reserves

Before this model is presented, it is necessary to give some precision to the terms 'international reserves' and 'international money' which have been used interchangeably at various times before in this text. International reserves are formally defined to be assets national governments are willing to accept from other national governments in settlement of debts. Because of this acceptability in international transactions between countries, governments are willing to accumulate these assets and use them as national 'reserves' against periods when aggregate payments to foreigners exceed aggregate receipts from them.

What are the characteristics of these assets countries are willing to use as reserves? As in the case of national moneys, the most important characteristic of the assets is that they are willingly accepted by others in payment of debts, and that there exists confidence in their future acceptability. This description of the characteristics of money differs from that found in textbooks a generation ago when there was a stress on the portability, scarcity, divisibility and durability of money. Some scholars maintained that the intrinsic value of the asset, its usefulness in other employments, was most important. These last characteristics do not catch the essential nature of money as well as does the simple proposition that money is what people accept as money. Thus, man's history abounds with cases where strange commodities have served as money, the immovable stones of Yap, beads, nuts, seashells, cows, cigarettes and pieces of paper. The fact that these commodities have at one time or the other been used as money does not mean that societies using them might not have been better off if they could have agreed on the use of some other commodity or instrument. As modern industrial economies developed, it was in fact recognized that society had a conscious option as to the instrument the public would use as money.

Historically, most of the money instruments were produced in the economy. Their production required scarce resources, which were thus not available for the production of goods and services for consumption or investment. Gold and silver, the commodities with the most widespread use as money in the past, had to be dug out of the ground at great cost in terms of labour and capital. The recognition that pieces of paper and cheap metal carrying the government's seal and that book entries reflecting transfer of assets could do the job as well as these produced commodities gave rise to the widespread use of paper money, fractional coins of little intrinsic value, bank cheques and demand deposits. These government-issued types of money became known as fiat money, and the commodity substitutes produced by the private banking system were named credit money. They both permit society to have an efficient financial system without requiring the expenditures of real resources as does commodity money.

What is true for national economies is also true for the international monetary relations. The family of nations has the conscious choice of making international money what it wants that money to be. This is the essential point implicit in the modern definition of money as assets that are acceptable as means of payment. If countries agree that they will accept only gold, then gold will be the international money. But if countries also are willing to receive payment in the form of claims exchangeable for gold, then these claims will be money, either alone or together with the gold itself. Naturally, fiat or credit money can similarly become the only form in which national monetary reserves are held and inter-country debts are settled.

Since the end of the Second World War the world's reserves have been gold, national currencies exchangeable for gold, most notably dollars and sterling, and credit with the International Monetary Fund. Other potential forms of international reserve assets will be discussed in the following chapters.

Before closing this analysis of the nature and cost of 'money', it has to be pointed out that in one important respect the fiat and credit moneys, both national and international, are different from the commodity moneys. While the supply of commodity money is regulated by market-forces and ideally requires no government intervention, the fiat and credit moneys involve governments in the issue and surveillance of its supply. These government activities in the monetary field result in some very important and difficult problems which the market tends to solve automatically. For persons who like the social and economic consequences resulting from unmitigated market forces and who distrust the wisdom, if not the intentions, of government decision makers in the sphere of economics, this characteristic of commodity money represents a great advantage compensating in full for the greater social cost of producing commodity rather than fiat or credit money. Conversely, there are persons who feel that the market left alone has resulted in socially undesirable patterns of income and consumption and has caused so many costly instabilities in employment and growth that they welcome the opportunity to issue fiat money and regulate the quantity of credit money. For individuals who hold these views, the lower social cost of producing fiat and credit money merely is an added advantage of that form of money.

This brief discussion of the nature of international reserves already had to refer to value judgements about income distributions, the fallibility of the market, and the wisdom of economic policy makers. Value judgements like these will appear repeatedly in the subsequent discussions although an effort will be made to keep them separate from more objectively measurable performance characteristics of alternative forms of world monetary order. However, their recognition and appreciation is one important part of understanding the choices facing society and why negotiations for world monetary reform are essentially political in nature.

Exchange Rate Flexibility and the Demand for Reserves

The working of the international monetary system will be discussed through the analysis of an abstract institution called the 'market' for international reserves, represented by Figure 1. It is very similar to the 'market' for money found in the conventional Keynesian analysis of the speculative demand for cash. The horizontal axis measures the quantity of the world's reserves demanded or supplied at any given moment in time. However, in contrast with the Keynesian analysis, the demand for and supply of reserves are not shown to be primarily a function of the interest rate, but of a variable called 'exchange rate flexibility'. This variable is shown in the vertical axis of Figure 1 and must be thought of as an index of national exchange rate adjustments. An empirical measure of this index would contain as a basic ingredient the number of all exchange rate changes that have occured over a given period in the past. The construction of the index would involve weighting each change by the size of the rate adjustment and the size of the foreign-trade sector of the countries involved. As will become clearer in the following discussions, however, it is not so much the past exchange rate adjustments with which this analysis is concerned as it is with the willingness of countries to solve future balance of payments problems through exchange rate adjustments rather than restrictions on trade, income changes, domestic price changes or some other methods. Infinity in the index of exchange rate flexibility is assumed to be equivalent to the complete absence of all government intervention in the foreign exchange markets so that rates are entirely free to find their own equilibrium levels.

The choice of having the index of flexibility on the vertical axis indicates the relative importance attached to this variable in the present analysis as a determinant of the demand for reserves, just as having the interest rate on the vertical axis in graphs depicting the money market focuses the attention on its importance for the determination of

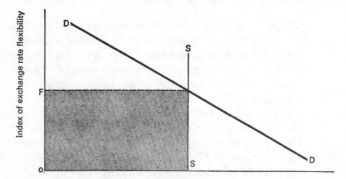

Figure 1. Aggregate world reserves demanded and supplied

equilibrium in that market. However, as is well known, the equilibrium values of the interest rate and quantity of money demanded are determined by a set of other variables, or *ceteris paribus* conditions, such as tastes, incomes, the relative prices of rival and complementary goods, factor costs, etc. as well as the interest rate. In fact, it is changes in these underlying conditions which cause the demand and supply curves to shift and result in the appearance of temporary conditions of 'excess demand' or 'excess supply' until new equilibrium relationships have been established in the market. In the analysis of the market for international reserves the *ceteris paribus* conditions, such as the propensity to adjust domestic prices and incomes, impose tariffs, etc., are very important and the analysis in chapter 3 will be concerned with how changes in them affect the demand for reserves. Therefore, the initial focus of the analysis on exchange rate flexibility must be interpreted as being primarily a heuristic device focusing attention on the very important interrelation between exchange rate adjustments and the demand for reserves, leading logically into the subsequent discussion of other determinants of this demand for reserves.

The Supply Curve

For purposes of the present analysis, it is convenient to assume that the quantity of reserves available to the world during any time period is exogenously given at O S, so that the supply curve is the vertical line S S shown in Figure 1. This assumption is most realistic if reserves consist of a commodity, such as gold, or if some central authority regulates the quantity of international fiat or credit money in existence, since neither of these magnitudes are influenced by nations' willingness to adjust their exchange rates. In traditional national income analysis it is also normally assumed that the quantity of money is exogenously given and the similarity of the assumption in the two frameworks is obvious.

The assumption of a constant supply of reserves is not realistic under the gold exchange standard where some national currencies are used as international reserves, since the quantity of these reserves in existence depends on the size and duration of the deficits incurred by the countries serving as the world's bankers. If these countries are willing to eliminate balance of payments deficits through devaluation, then the supply of reserves is smaller the greater their readiness to do so. The supply curve consequently would slope downward from left to right. However, the assumption of a constant supply of reserves will be retained for simplicity in spite of its lack of realism under the gold exchange standard. Any other assumptions would merely complicate the analysis without adding to its value.

The Demand Curve

The demand curve D D shown in Figure 1 indicates the relationship between the aggregate quantity of reserves countries wish to hold and the degree to which exchange rates are flexible. As can be seen, the demand curve slopes downward and to the right, thus implying that the greater the exchange rate flexibility the smaller the demand for reserves. The logical and empirical relevance of this particular functional relationship will be justified with the aid of a simple model.

Consider the foreign exchange market of country A as shown in Figure 2. Abstracting from all private capital movements, both long and short-term, speculative and normal, the demand for foreign exchange (D_0D_0) is due to the fact that the population in A wishes to acquire goods and services from the rest of the world, which for the sake of simplicity is assumed to consist of one country B. The greater the price of country B's currency the more expensive are that country's products for the residents of A and the smaller is the quantity of foreign exchange demanded. The supply curve of foreign exchange (S_0S_0) in

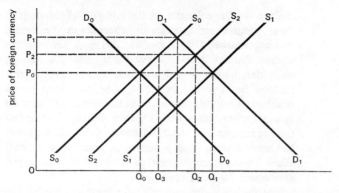

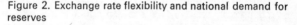

Figure 2. Exchange rate flexibility and national demand for reserves

Figure 2 is analogously derived from country B's demand for the goods and services produced in country A. The higher the price of foreign exchange from the point of view of country A, the cheaper is that country's domestic currency and output for foreigners and therefore the more of their own currency is supplied by foreigners in the process of purchasing A's output.[1]

Initially the foreign exchange market is in equilibrium at the rate OP_0 and at a trade of OQ_0 foreign currency per time period. Now assume that this equilibrium is disturbed through a change in taste, technology, differential rates of income growth or inflation, such that the demand for foreign exchange in country A shifts from D_0D_0 to D_1D_1 while the supply curve remains unchanged. The discussion of *ceteris paribus* conditions in the next

1. The slope of the supply curve shown in Figure 1 implies that country A's excess demand curve for country B's products expressed in foreign currency is not perfectly inelastic. Similarly, the slope of the demand curve indicates that country B's excess demand curve for country A's exports has an elasticity greater than one, expressed in foreign currency. The analysis of the foreign markets underlying this diagram is well known from the detailed discussions of the Marshall–Lerner condition. See, for example, the textbooks by Kindleberger (1963) and Meade (1951).

chapter dwells at length on the nature and duration of these disequilibrating shifts of schedules in the foreign exchange market. For the moment it is most convenient to assume that the demand curve shifts upward as shown, stays there for one period, and then returns to its original position for a period before shifting downward by an equal amount for the duration of another period and so on in a cycle. In order to keep Figure 2 simple, only the first third of the cycle, i.e. the upward shift of the demand curve has been shown. Such a pattern of shifts may be considered as reflecting seasonal or cyclical variations in real net demand for foreign products.

The theory of the international adjustment mechanism suggests that a disturbance, such as the initial outward shift of the demand curve to D_1D_1, leads to internal changes in relative factor and product prices and movement of factors which cause automatic adjusting shifts in the supply and demand curves. Consider, for example, a sudden shift in country A's demand away from domestically to foreign produced automobiles. The resultant decrease in the demand for A's automobiles tends to lower their prices, inducing consumers to substitute A's automobiles for B's, and resulting in a shift of the demand curve back toward its initial position by a magnitude depending on demand and supply elasticities but never quite equal to the initial shift. Unemployed resources from the automobile industry tend to move into country A's export industry, increasing supply and resulting in a shift of the supply curve for foreign exchange downward and to the right. In long run equilibrium the change in country A's taste may or may not result in a new price of foreign currency, which in models like the present one stands for the country's 'terms of trade', the rate at which domestic and foreign products are exchanged.[2]

2. The qualitative, long run effects of given disturbances to equilibrium depend on the shape of the domestic and foreign Marshallian offer curves, which in turn depend on tastes, technology, and factor availability. See Kindleberger (1963) and Meade (1951) for an analysis of these interrelationships.

It is now assumed that domestic factor and commodity prices in country A are rather inflexible in the downward direction and that the flow of resources between industries is very slow. Consequently, the adjustment mechanism works only with a considerable lag and, for purposes of the present analysis, will be assumed not to work at all. Such an assumption may well be realistic in the context of short-lived seasonal and cyclical disturbances to equilibrium.

In this model the governments of both countries are assumed to have the option of entering into the foreign exchange market by buying or selling foreign exchange as they desire. Such intervention is represented by a shift in the appropriate schedule. For example, if country A decides to sell foreign exchange the supply schedule is shifted outward from S_0S_0 to S_1S_1 as shown in Figure 2. It is clear that if country A sells foreign currency it must be able to deliver it to the buyers and must either own it or acquire it somewhere. It is reasonable to assume that each of the countries owns a stock of gold which can be exchanged for the currency of the other country, which can then be used for the market intervention. Analogously, it can be assumed that when a country acquires foreign exchange by entering the market as a purchaser, it immediately presents this currency to the other country for payment in gold. It is worth pointing out, however, that in a two-country model the appreciation of one currency means the depreciation of the other. Consequently, neither country ever has to purchase foreign currency to avoid appreciation as long as the other country prevents the depreciation of its own currency.

Now consider the demand for gold as a function of the flexibility of exchange rates when the exchange market is subject to the cyclical pattern of demand variation postulated above. At one extreme, the greatest variance of exchange rates over a full cycle is found when the rate is free to find its own level without any government intervention. Since the governments need to hold no gold if they do not intervene, this greatest flexibility of rates is associated with zero world demand for reserves.

At the other extreme, zero variation in exchange rates results when the governments peg the rate at OP_0 and meet the excess demand Q_0Q_1 by obtaining foreign currency for gold from their stock piles. The maximum quantity of gold needed is Q_0Q_1 since the excess demand has been assumed to persist for one period. At the end of the cycle, country A's stock of gold is back at its initial level since it purchases foreign currency, and exchanges it for gold during the third phase of the cycle when the demand-curve is shifted downward below D_0D_0 (not shown in the graph), resulting in a price equal to $OP_0 - P_0P_1$.

In between these two extremes of complete flexibility and absolute rigidity in rates, is the arrangement where the government of A lets its currency depreciate somewhat, say to OP_2, after the outward shift of the demand curve has occurred. Under these circumstances the market's excess demand for foreign exchange to be met from the reserve of gold is equal to Q_3Q_2. Since $Q_3Q_2 < Q_0Q_1$, the stock of gold required is smaller in the case when the exchange rate is free to fluctuate somewhat, than if the government keeps it pegged rigidly.

From these three discrete cases it is possible to generalize that the demand for gold is smaller the more flexible the exchange rates. In terms of Figure 1 this generalization, and the preceding analysis on which it is based, justify the slope of the demand curve downward and to the right. The position of the demand curve in space of Figure 1 and the points at which it touches the axes are determined by the model's assumptions about the nature and length of the demand cycle. Thus, under the preceding specifications there was a maximum of four exchange rate changes which resulted in a zero need for gold holdings, and defined a unique point at which the demand curve touches the vertical axis. Similarly at zero flexibility the quantity of reserves demanded is uniquely determined at Q_0Q_1.

It is easy to work out the relationship between these points on the axes and the assumptions about the duration and magnitude of each cycle.

Next is an analysis of the implications which different sets of assumptions about the disturbances of equilibrium have for the demand for reserves. The most important deficiency of the preceding cycle analysis of disturbances is its assumed perfect periodicity. Under these circumstances it would be highly unlikely that in the real world the exchange rates also would fluctuate in a perfect cycle, even in the absence of government intervention, simply because private speculators would buy foreign exchange when the price is low and sell when the price is high. In perfect markets and under perfect predictability the actions of these private speculators would permit only marginal deviations of the exchange rate from the cycle averages.[3] In fact, it is well known that even in the absence of certainty, speculators in commodities and exchange markets tend to average out seasonal variations in demand and supply.

In order to overcome this lack of realism in the preceding set of assumptions about the behaviour of foreign exchange rates, a model is introduced where private speculators cannot profit consistently as a result of the assumption that the shifts in the demand and supply schedules are purely random, producing a pattern of prices equal to a random walk without a drift. The basic nature of the random walk can be explained most easily by postulating that each price change is of equal size and that one change takes place each period. The absence of drift implies that tomorrow's price change has a probability of one-half to be

3. In terms of the modern theory of forward exchange, the forward demand-supply schedule of speculators would be perfectly elastic at the expected spot rate. Interest arbitrators would then tend to move spot funds in such quantities as to force equalization of interest rates and of the current spot rates with the expected spot rate, which is assumed to be equal to the forward rate. Thus, in this world of certain future prices interest and forward rates would be equal everywhere and all fluctuations would be eliminated. For a detailed analysis of the forward exchange market see Grubel (1966) and Stoll (1968).

up and one-half to be down, regardless of past price behaviour.

These assumptions work out to produce the following probable exchange rates in future periods. At time period zero the price of exchange is P_0. There is an equal chance $(0·5)$ that in period one the price is $P_0 + 1$ or that it is $P_0 - 1$. In period two the price has an equal chance of being $P_0 + 2$ or P_0 if in the first period it had moved to $P_0 + 1$. If on the other hand the price had been $P_0 - 1$ in period one, then the period two price has an equal probability of being P_0 or $P_0 - 2$. The price in period three depends on what happened in the preceding periods, etc., as can be seen schematically in the following:

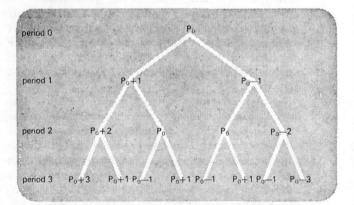

Figure 3. Random walk model of reserve changes

The most important conclusion from this model is that the probability of very large future cumulative price deviations in one direction is never zero since the left and right extremities of the chain increase with the length of the chain. The probability of three consecutive price decreases in three periods is $(0·5)^3$. In general, the probability of future maximum price changes in each period i is $\text{Pr (max L)}_i = (0·5)^i$.

Now consider the implications of this random walk model for the demand for reserves by assuming that the adverse event in each period is represented by a shift of the demand curve from D_0D_0 to D_1D_1 in Figure 4, resulting in an increase in the price of foreign currency equal to one. Official intervention represented by an outward shift of the supply curve from S_0S_0 to S_1S_1 results in a loss of reserves equal to 1. At the end of the first period it is assumed that the adjustment mechanism discussed above causes an outward shift of the country's market supply of

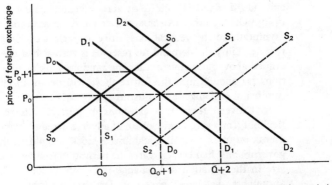

Figure 4. Random disturbances, exchange rate changes and the demand for reserves

foreign exchange schedule, also from S_0S_0 to S_1S_1 or in a return of the demand curve to its original position D_0D_0. At the beginning of the next period a second adverse shift of the demand schedule is assumed to take place and is represented by the shift of the schedule D_0D_0 to D_1D_1 or D_1D_1 to D_2D_2. Again official stabilization of the exchange rate requires the use of one unit of reserves (S_1S_1). The adjustment mechanism working with a lag again eliminates the need for intervention in the third period by causing a shift of the supply curve from S_1S_1 to S_2S_2 or of the demand curve from D_1D_1 to D_0D_0. However, in the third period the events of the preceding periods are repeated and so on in an infinite series leading to an infinitely large demand for reserves. The same results are attained if the adjustment lag is assumed to be shorter or longer than in the present model except that when it is assumed to be zero then the demand for reserves is also zero. In general, a given pattern of disturbances over any given time period requires fewer reserves, the more rapid and complete the adjustment mechanism.

Under these assumptions, then, the demand curve for reserves in Figure 1 becomes asymptotic to the horizontal axis, i.e. demand is infinite at zero exchange rate flexibility.[4] On the other extreme, the demand curve becomes asymptotic to the vertical axis, since at perfect exchange rate flexibility the demand for reserves is zero as had been argued above, and since under the random walk assumptions far enough into the future there will be an infinite number of exchange rate adjustments.

In between these two extremes of perfect and zero flexibility, any given finite chain of adverse demand movements requires a smaller stabilizing stock of gold in the governments' hands the greater the permitted frequency or size in the variation of exchange rates, by reason of the arguments developed above under the assumption of cyclical disturbances but equally applicable under the present assumptions about the randomness of disturbances. How far away from the origin the demand curve is located depends on the size of random disturbances,

4. In the real world demand would never be infinite for two reasons. First, large and persistent reserve losses can always be met by devaluation as well as income and price level changes and direct controls on international trade. Second, reserves are not a free good. Their acquisition requires the surrender of real resources. How many resources each country is willing to give up depends on its attitudes towards the risk of running out of reserves and having to use exchange rate, income, price and other adjustments. Given the probability distribution of losses at any given point in the future, which can be calculated from the random-walk model, given the real costs of making these adjustments, and the opportunity cost of reserves, each country holds as many reserves as it considers optimum after discounting of the future, uncertain losses at a rate appropriate for its own tastes. See the last part of chapter 3 for an elaboration of this analysis.

which in the real world are not of equal size as hypothesized in the model, as well as on a host of other conditions to be discussed in the next chapter.

However, before turning to these conditions it is necessary to go a little more deeply into the nature of the demand for reserves to find out whether from the point of view of world welfare each point on the demand curve is equally desirable. In order to do so, it is useful to continue the assumption about the randomness of exogenous disturbances in the international markets.

Uncertainty about future prices represents a disutility to consumers and producers. When prices fluctuate, consumers cannot be certain either about their standard of living tomorrow or whether they have to readjust their preferred patterns of consumption. Producers in capitalist societies have to pay fixed prices for labour and other factors of production at the time they are required in the production process. With uncertain prices for the final product in the future, the profitability of manufacture is established only when the product has finally been sold. Similar disadvantages exist for the lenders and borrowers of capital. The market tends to provide institutions which reduce this uncertainty of future prices, such as future markets and speculation, but these institutions in turn absorb resources and increase the cost of producing a given amount of output. Fluctuating exchange rates and international trade are themselves important sources of uncertainty, frequently not caused by real disturbances in the specific markets relevant for the producer or consumer. For example, the user of imported raw materials faces added uncertainty about his cost of production if exchange rates are free to fluctuate in response to real disturbances in the demand or supply of other traded commodities. For these reasons it is true that stability of exchange rates is preferable to instability, everything else remaining the same.[5]

5. These arguments about the cost of uncertainty are examined critically for their empirical importance in chapter 6.

Logically it follows from this argument about the cost of exchange rate instability that perfect exchange rigidity is optimum. However, the maintenance of such rigidity itself bears a cost. As has been shown above with the help of the basic model, such rigidity necessitates the holding of large quantities of reserves and requires that the surplus country be ready to accept them in return for the transfer of real resources whenever exogeneous disturbances cause large cumulative disequilibria. These characteristics make for a typical economic problem: one benefit can be attained only at the expense of reducing another and countries therefore face a trade-off between the benefits from greater exchange rate stability, on the one hand, and the benefits (lower cost) of holding fewer reserves, on the other. One of the main issues in the discussion of international monetary order is exactly about the optimum degree of exchange rate flexibility in the light of existing disturbances to equilibrium. Thus, in Figure 1, the available supply of reserves at O S implies an exchange rate stability index of O F. In this framework the basic issue is whether an increase in reserves is desirable given the benefits from greater price stability, versus the cost of holding more reserves and being forced to lend real resources in return for them. An empirical answer to this question involves the rather technical problems of measuring the gains from stability and cost of reserve holding as well as the even more difficult problem of measuring the welfare losses caused by countries which are forced to accept monetary assets and lend to the rest of the world even though they would rather not.

In the real world the task of quantifying these effects is complicated still further because the trade-off just discussed is only one of many. The social choice of world monetary organization in the framework of the present model involves not only shifts in the supply curve, but also shifts in the demand curve for reserves. The next chapter turns to an analysis of factors causing the demand curve to shift up or down.

3 Other Determinants of the Demand for Reserves

The following discussion in this chapter is broken down into several distinct parts, each of which deals with a set of closely related determinants of the aggregate demand for international reserves.

Propensity to Make Domestic Adjustments

In the preceding analysis the assumption was made that governments did not interfere with the shifts in the demand or supply schedules in the foreign exchange markets and that instead they restricted their stabilizing efforts to keeping the exchange rate unchanged through the sale or purchase of foreign exchange, which is equivalent to adding a constant amount to the market demand or supply schedules. The following analysis introduces the assumption that governments are able and willing to engage in domestic price, income, tariff and other policies which result in shifts of the demand and supply curves in the foreign exchange market. For example, consider that a change in taste by the residents of country A causes the country's demand schedule for foreign exchange to shift upward and to the right from $D_0 D_0$ to $D_1 D_1$ in Figure 2. The implementation of the appropriate domestic policies in country A can prevent any change in the existing exchange rate from taking place by causing the demand curve to move down again, the supply curve to move up, or both.

Thus, exchange rate stability can be attained without the use of any foreign exchange by the government. In more general terms, the greater the countries' propensity to use policies which influence the economy's foreign exchange demand and supply, the smaller is the demand for international reserves. In the analytical framework of Figure 1, this relationship implies that the demand curve for international reserves moves closer to the origin the greater the countries' propensity to use these policies. In the extreme, when countries are willing to use these policies with whatever intensity necessary to neutralize all disturbances in the foreign exchange market instantaneously, exchange rates remain stable and the demand curve for international reserves vanishes.

What are the domestic policies which can perform this service and what are the costs and benefits from using them? These policies are well known to students of international economics and of the problems of balance of payments adjustments. Therefore, they will be discussed here only briefly under the headings of price and income adjustments and tariffs and direct controls.

Price and Income Adjustments

Classical economists used to stress the role of prices in the determination of balance of payments. Thus, country A which was normally assumed to be at full employment can improve its balance of payments by lowering its domestic price level, assuming the Marshall–Lerner conditions are met. Lower prices in country A reduce its residents' demand for foreign products (demand curve for foreign exchange shifts down and to the left) while the rest of the world finds country A a more attractive place to buy (supply curve shifts down and to the left). It is obvious how these results of domestic price decreases can be used to neutralize the disturbing outward shift of the demand curve hypothesized above to any degree desired by the appropriate change in the domestic price level.

While classical economists discussed the role of prices in balance of payments determination, the Keynesian revolution led to the emphasis of the relationship between income changes and the balance of payments. When countries are at a level below full employment (with prices normally assumed to be stable), then any change in the level of employment and income is accompanied by a change in imports in the same direction and by a magnitude determined by the country's 'marginal propensity to import.' Thus, if country A's income decreases by one million dollars and the marginal propensity to import is one tenth, then imports go down by a hundred thousand dollars. In the analytical framework of Figure 2, such a decrease in imports due to a change in income is represented by a shift of the demand curve downward and to the left. This shift in the demand curve may be partially offset by a shift of the supply curve upward, and to the left because country A's decreased demand for products from the rest of the world is likely to reduce income there and consequently the demand for A's products. In spite of these repercussions, however, a country can normally find one determinate level of income at which its foreign payments are balanced at the given exchange rate.

As part of the synthesis between classical and Keynesian economics during the 1950s, domestic price and income changes were linked empirically and theoretically in a concept now known as the Phillips curve. It shows, as in Figure 5, that in capitalist economies generally, annual rates of price increases are greater the lower the rate of unemployment. This linkage between employment and prices makes it possible to discuss together the social costs of using changes in these variables as a method to stabilize the exchange market.[1]

Consider, for example, the initial situation where the rest of the world has a stable price level and country A also has attained price stability at three per cent unemployment. Now country A experiences the changes in taste and the shift of the foreign exchange demand curve upward and to the right hypothesized above, which

[1]. For some recent arguments challenging the validity of the Phillips curve concept see Phelps (1967) and Friedman (1968).

according to classical reasoning can be compensated for by a decrease in the price level. The Phillips curve analysis implies that any effort of lowering the rate at which the price level changes, through a reduction in the supply of money in the classical manner, will be accompanied by a

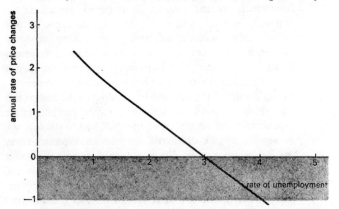

Figure 5. The Phillips curve trade-off between unemployment and price stability

reduction in income. At the same time, any reduction in income achieved in the Keynesian manner, through the use of restrictive monetary or fiscal policy, also causes a lowering of the rate of price increases. Thus, because of the price–income linkage the balance of payments improves as a result of both the lowering of income and the price level.[2]

The social cost of using domestic price and income changes for the achievement of stable exchange rates takes the form of foregone national income resulting from

2. It is worth pointing out here the implication of the fact that the vertical axis in the Phillips curve diagram measures the *annual* rate of price changes. As a result, the raising of unemployment from 3 to 4 per cent implies a decrease of country A's price level relative to that in the rest of the world of 1 per cent each year, or 5 per cent in five years, etc. Because of these cumulative price level effects even substantial disequilibria can be corrected at relatively small sacrifices in employment per year, as long as the adjustment is permitted to take place over a reasonably long period of time.

the lower level of employment. This reduction of income can be expressed in terms of dollars by a set of calculations which takes account of man-hours lost, lower productivity of capital, smaller labour-force participation, etc. But the higher unemployment also causes welfare losses in the form of frustration and loss of dignity experienced by those willing but unable to work, which the output calculations fail to reveal. Somewhat off-setting this calculation is the appropriate consideration of the value of leisure enjoyed by at least a part of those refusing to accept low-paying jobs offered to them.

In the nineteenth century and before, countries have been quite willing to let domestic price and income changes bear a significant part of the burden of adjustment to disturbances of external equilibrium. Most often these domestic adjustments occurred simply because governments failed to offset the automatic forces generated by the internal disequilibria, which led to gold losses and reductions in the money supply. However, as industrialization proceeded and the welfare losses from unemployment became more pronounced and as the trade-off between price stability and unemployment became steeper, countries became increasingly less willing to make domestic price and income adjustments. Since the end of the Second World War the maintenance of full employment has become one of the most important responsibilities of national governments and income changes for the sake of external equilibrium have been made only rarely.

However, occasionally countries do lower incomes to balance their payments. Reference has already been made to the income reductions undertaken by the British government in 1966 and in other years. Presumably in these cases the British government decided that the welfare losses from this action were smaller than those that would have accompanied a devaluation of sterling, the resultant loss of national prestige and the potential danger to the existing world payments system. By the same standards of judgement, the 1967 devaluation of sterling seemed to indicate that balance-of-payments adjustment through domestic policies sufficiently restrictive to work was not possible, presumably because of the political repercussions of severe unemployment and cut-back of domestic government expenditures undertaken by a Labour government. At the time of writing this book a definitive interpretation of the causes of the 1967 devaluation had not been made.

Tariffs and Direct Controls

Domestic price and employment policies leave it to the free market mechanism to select specific industries, groups of capitalists and labourers, who bear the cost of adjustment to external disturbances. Thus, for example, domestic restriction of demand through high interest rates appears to cause normally a disproportionately larger reduction in the construction of residential houses than in most other sectors of the economy. Such a slowdown in residential construction, unemployment of workers in this industry and its suppliers may be considered inconsistent with other national objectives of social welfare. For this reason, governments often find it politically convenient to use more direct policies, such as the imposition of tariffs or direct controls, to achieve the desired shift of the demand and supply curves in the foreign exchange markets without having to sacrifice the other social objectives.

The use of tariffs and direct controls is politically more convenient because, first, the resultant welfare losses are widely distributed throughout the economy and most often the losers are not effectively organized to lobby for their interests. For example, when tariffs on textile imports are raised to shift down country A's demand curve for foreign exchange and return it to its equilibrium position, the welfare losses of the consumers of textiles having to pay higher prices are widely dispersed and only marginal. An elected government most probably loses fewer votes as a result of the price increase in textiles than it would from a pronounced depression in the housing industry, where the tariff and the income reduction are assumed to have the same effect on the demand for foreign exchange.

Second, the use of tariffs and direct controls often benefits specific and highly organized groups of capitalists and labourers. These groups such as the producers of textiles, steel, oil, etc., quite frequently have a long-standing and traditional demand before the government that their industries be protected from foreign imports for a variety of reasons, the most popular of which are that the industry is in its infancy, that foreign labour is exploited and the resultant competition is 'unfair', that the industry's output is needed for national defence, etc. While governments normally resist the pressures from these groups, at times when serious balance-of-payments deficits persist these arguments often provide ready-made rationalizations to reduce imports in the politically most expedient fashion.

Since the 1930s countries in the industrialized West and elsewhere have become very expert in influencing imports and exports through the imposition of tariffs and direct controls. While the international agreements made after the Second World War, most notably those of Bretton Woods and the General Agreements on Tariffs and Trade, made some methods of control 'illegal', among them multiple exchange rates and discriminatory tariffs, ingenious administrators had no difficulties in devising new methods that were outwardly respectable. In the United States the last decade saw the imposition of 'voluntary' restraints on the imports of foreign textiles and on the export of U.S. portfolio capital and direct investments, the interest 'equalization' tax, the reduction of duty-free import allowances for tourists, the order to government agencies that they could purchase foreign products, only if they were priced at 60 per cent below the U.S. substitutes, the strict enforcement of sanitary and other rules on quality, labelling, etc., which discriminated against foreign imports, and others. The United Kingdom imposed 'temporary' surcharges on imports and imposed wage and price freezes. Western European countries in which value-added and turnover taxes are important revenue sources manipulate refunds of those to exporters and provide other subsidies, as through insurance schemes. Under-developed countries have constructed complex systems of tariffs, direct controls on imports and subsidies to exporters and producers of import subsidies.

While these methods of influencing balance of payments are politically expedient for governments to undertake, they are likely to result in losses of efficiency and welfare both nationally and through the non-optimal international division of labour. Thus, while the use of price and employment policies and of tariffs and direct controls reduces the demand for international reserves and the need for exchange rate flexibility, this advantage is gained at a cost. However, since the use of exchange rate adjustments and reserves to correct international disequilibria each are costly also as has been discussed in chapter 2, the world economy may be best served if countries are willing to use domestic adjustments to some degree. Theoretically, the efficient policy mix would use reserves, exchange rate flexibility, tariff policies and domestic adjustments with such intensity that the loss of world welfare from the marginal use of each would be equal.

While it is easy to state these efficiency criteria theoretically, it is not possible to set out empirical measures with the tools of analysis available to economists at the present. This inability to produce scientifically valid empirical measures of welfare losses gives rise to many disagreements among men who substitute intuitive judgements for them, which usually seem to be coloured by self-interest, either consciously or unconsciously. In chapter 4 the most important of these disagreements will be discussed.

World Economic Stability and Co-operation Among Nations

Since national governments have engaged in full employment policies many of the balance of payments disequilibria experienced by countries of the Western World have not been caused by what previously had been considered 'random' disturbances, but instead by conflicting national policies. When one country decides that it is socially optimum to operate at such a low level of unemployment that its annual rate of price increases is 5 per cent while the rest of the world operates at an annual rate of 3 per cent price increases, then balance of payments disequilibria appear. These kinds of disequilibria require the same types of adjustments and reserve holdings as do those caused by random disturbances. However, while random shocks by definition cannot be foreseen or avoided, the policy-caused disturbances can be reduced by the proper co-ordination of national policies at the international level. Such co-ordination, even if it takes place only at informal meetings of finance ministers and if it is without any enforcement mechanism for passed resolutions, can reduce the frequency of these types of disequilibria and thus the need for international reserves.

In the preceding example it was assumed that the source of the disturbance was the existence of different national tastes for unemployment and the rate of inflation. In the real world, however, another cause of disturbances is that such economic policies are not made with great precision. Countries may aim for certain rates of inflation and unemployment, but these are achieved only with varying degrees of success, partly because of the existence of random shocks to domestic stability, partly because of the inadequacy of policy makers and instruments, and partly because of unknown economic influences from abroad. While the adequacy of policy makers and instruments cannot be improved except by the time-consuming accumulation of scientific and practical evidence, the importance of disturbing influences from abroad can be reduced by co-operation among nations, which regularly inform each other of pending policy actions in their own countries. Co-operation and international consultation, thus, can help to harmonize national economic targets and reduce the uncertainty surrounding their achievement. Both of these effects tend to lower the frequency and intensity of disturbances to international equilibrium. Therefore, the greater the co-operation among nations, the smaller the demand for international reserves needed for stabilization of foreign exchange markets.

Co-operation, however, is likely to lead to additional benefits. First, in the basic model constructed in chapter 2, it had been assumed that country A could obtain national currencies for intervention only through the exchange of gold. Now if country B were willing to give country A the needed exchange not only for gold but also in return for A's general obligation, then the availability of this credit would enable country A to get along with less gold. Co-operation among nations on other economic matters tends to create the understanding that the mutual extension of such credits is beneficial to all and the general atmosphere of working together tends to lead to the enactment of practical programmes of stand-by credits, etc., and thus a lowering of the demand for actual reserves.

Second, co-operation among nation states with close cultural and ethical ties tends to pave the road for ultimate economic integration with common currencies, free factor movements, etc. Such integration leads to a pooling of national reserve assets and may reduce the need for them. The latter result occurs if the larger geographic area of the integrated unit encompasses a wider variety of agricultural and industrial production than was the case in each of the smaller component nations. The greater variety of output increases the probability that a depression in one industry and a poor harvest in one region is offset by a boom in another industry and bumper harvest in another region, thus preventing a balance-of-payments surplus or deficit that would have occurred if the industries and regions belonged to different countries. The logically extreme benefits from this kind of diversification are reached when the entire world is integrated into one 'country', since the world as a whole can never have any balance-of-payments deficits.

Since the end of the Second World War, co-operation among the industrialized nations of the West has increased almost continuously. The most significant early step on this road has been the co-operative distribution of Marshall Plan aid by the countries of Western Europe. During the same period nations learned to work together in the institutions set up under the Bretton Woods Agreements, especially the International Monetary Fund. Other international organizations with more limited memberships such as the Organization for Economic Co-operation and Development were set up. The Bank for International Settlement in Basle, Switzerland, an institution for international monetary co-operation that had survived the Second World War and had served the League of Nations, became a centre for close consultations among the so-called Group of Ten (Belgium, Canada, France, Germany, Italy, Japan, Netherlands, Sweden, United Kingdom, United States). In recent years the Finance Ministers of these countries have been meeting once every month (except in August and September) in Basle to discuss international monetary problems, the creation and expansion of credit facilities, and how to avoid inconsistent national policies. The formation of the Benelux Union, the European Economic Community, and the European Free Trade Area has resulted in exceedingly close co-operation among the members of each association and the European Economic Community appears to be making continued, if uneven, progress toward complete economic integration.

In terms of the basic analytical framework, increased co-operation among national economic policy makers and actual economic integration through the surrender of some national sovereignty to supra-national authorities tend to reduce the frequency and intensity of disturbing shifts of demand and supply curves in foreign exchange markets. They thus reduce the need to hold international reserves used to stabilize the exchange rates.

However, as in the case of all the other policies influencing the need to hold reserves, such benefits are acquired at a social cost. In nearly all civilizations man has given strong evidence that he desires to have the right to be different from others, to be an individual with his own identity and tastes. Nations similarly value highly their sovereignty and the right and opportunity for their citizens to enjoy life in ways most appropriate for them, their cultural, religious and economic backgrounds. Co-operation and integration among nations for the sake of the attainment of international objectives of necessity occasionally give rise to conflicts and countries have to sacrifice some of their rights to be different or have the rest of the world behave in ways most desirable to them. These sacrifices represent the social cost of using more co-operation and integration to reduce the demand for international reserves, the need for exchange rate flexibility, and for prices and income adjustments.

As in the previous analysis, efficient operation of the world monetary order requires that international co-operation be pushed to the point where at the margin the loss in welfare is just equal to that experienced by the marginal increase in the use of the other policy instruments.

Private Short-Term Capital Movements

Up to this point the analysis has abstracted from private short-term capital movements. These capital flows play an important role in the classical analysis of the international adjustment mechanism and their availability can reduce or increase the official demand for reserves. In order to see how private short-term capital flows can reduce the demand for reserves, it is useful to assume at first that exchange rates are absolutely fixed so that private entrepreneurs are motivated to move their funds only in response to actual interest rate differentials, not expected capital gains from exchange rate adjustments.

Consider country A initially in international payments equilibrium when a random event shifts up permanently its demand curve for foreign exchange (as from D_0D_0 to D_1D_1 in Figure 2). One result of such a shift, neglected thus far in our analysis, accompanies the government's intervention in the exchange market. The public purchases the foreign exchange from the government through the surrender of domestic currency. Unless the monetary authorities neutralize the resultant decrease in domestic currency in the public's hands, country A's domestic money supply is reduced and interest rates go up. How far these rates rise in the absence of any action by the monetary authorities depends on the interest elasticity of the supply of foreign short-term capital. For example, if this elasticity is high, then a small rise in country A's interest rate attracts large quantities of foreign arbitrage capital. These private capital imports into country A increase the supply of country B's currency in the foreign exchange market, i.e. they shift the supply curve downward and to the right. If this shift is insufficient to neutralize the initial disequilibrating shift in the demand curve, the government of country A has to sell more gold or foreign exchange to keep the exchange rate pegged at its initial level in the next period, the money supply is reduced further and the interest rate rises some more, attracting more foreign interest arbitrage capital, etc., until in the end the exchange rate is stabilized and the deficit in the trade balance each period is matched by an equal sized capital inflow in each period.[3] It is clear that the total intervention in the exchange market is smaller the greater the flows of foreign interest arbitrage capital attracted for a given rise in country A's interest rate. In the extreme of perfectly elastic supply of foreign private funds only marginal sales of gold, marginal reductions in

3. It is clear that if the shift in the demand schedule is permanent and the adjustment mechanism does not work automatically, such capital inflows have to continue indefinitely as a compensation for the balance of payments deficit taking place in each period. For a detailed analysis of this problem involving stock-flow relationships see Grubel (1968).

the money supply and marginal increases in the interest rate are required to attain stability in the foreign exchange market.

In the classical model of international adjustments the process just described represents a cushion softening the impact of foreign disturbances without interfering with the basic adjustment itself. In the preceding example country A experienced an increase in the demand for foreign exchange which required a lowering of its domestic price level (or income, in Keynesian terms). The reduction in the money supply and rise in the interest rates, however small, accomplish exactly this adjustment. The flow of private capital permits the loss of gold, reduction in the money supply and rise in the interest rate to be smaller, and the domestic adjustment to be slower and less disruptive to the economy than it would have to be in the absence of the private capital flows. Furthermore, if the disturbances to equilibrium follow a random pattern as had been hypothesized in chapter 2, then most of the time the initial disturbance is eliminated by an offsetting development and basic resource shifts and other adjustments in A are not necessary at all.

In the modern world this classical model of the role of international short-term capital flows has to be modified for two reasons. First, national monetary authorities very rarely permit the foreign sector to influence domestic money supplies and interest rates simply because of the overwhelming importance of their responsibility to maintain full employment, as was discussed above. Thus, there exists a strong tendency for interest rate differentials to be determined by the domestic requirements of countries, and not by the size of external disequilibria and the interest elasticity of private funds. As a result, nonspeculative interest arbitrage flows frequently tend to aggravate rather than alleviate balance-of-payments disequilibria. To the extent that interest rate differentials result in greater balance-of-payments swings through the working of interest arbitraging short-term capital flows, capital movements are increasing rather than decreasing the demand for international reserves.[4]

In recent years several useful methods of dealing with the conflict between the use of interest rates for the attainment of both internal and external stability have been developed. Forward exchange intervention permits the creation of effective interest rate incentives different for foreign and domestic wealth holders. Policies of changing the yield curve, known as Operation Twist in the United States, are designed to keep short-term interest rates at levels appropriate for foreign balance, while long-term rates are set to encourage the right amount of domestic investment for the attainment of full employment. Fiscal policy is used to influence employment levels, leaving authorities to adjust interest rates for the sake of external equilibrium. These policy instruments have been used successfully in *reducing* the conflict between internal and external stability in several instances. However, they have not been able to *eliminate* it.

Second, in the real world, private short-term capital movements are motivated not only by the arbitrage of interest rate differentials, but also by expected capital value changes accompanying exchange rate valuations. If an investor shifts a million dollars from country A to country B, and one week later country A's exchange rate is devalued by 10 per cent, the investor can immediately repatriate his funds and record a capital gain equal to an annual rate of return of 520 per cent (10 per cent per week for 52 weeks, not compounded). It is easy to see from this example how even smaller revaluations and longer shifts can yield large annual yields which often dominate

4. It is worth noting that these interest arbitrage capital flows are not 'speculative' but 'normal' and are caused by observable covered or uncovered profit opportunities existing in the market. Co-ordination of interest rate policies among nations can prevent many of the disturbing short-term capital flows from taking place except when countries with cyclical unemployment also have balance of payments deficits and the countries with overemployment also have balance of payments surpluses. For a more detailed analysis of these points in the theory of international short-term capital movements see Grubel (1966, chapter 14).

observed interest rate differentials. Under these circumstances, the large quantities of internationally mobile private short-term funds, which are so beneficial in the classical model, can become a serious disturbing influence as they move rapidly from one country to the next in expectation of capital gains from currency revaluations. During the 1930s speculative capital moving about the world in this fashion has been likened to loose cargo in a ship's hull being tossed about by the sea. These speculative movements have added to basic instabilities in the exchange markets and may have forced devaluations which otherwise may not have been necessary.

Since the end of the Second World War both speculative and interest arbitraging private short-term capital movements on several occasions have been sudden and large, and were capable of disrupting the international payments mechanism. But because of the co-operation among countries they have been prevented from doing so. Under this co-operation, countries in balance-of-payments difficulties, due to capital outflows, have been lent reserves by countries in payments surplus and international organizations sufficient to keep their exchange rates stable, no matter how large the private speculation and how relatively small their owned stock of reserves. The United Kingdom, Italy and the United States have been the most notable beneficiaries from these kinds of credit arrangements in recent years, though the 1967 sterling devaluation has shown that such co-operation has finite limits.

In the framework of the basic analysis the existence of an efficient system of international private capital flows assures that any disturbance in the foreign exchange market, such as the outward shift of the demand curve, is compensated for by an appropriate capital movement, which, for example, causes a shift in the supply curve. If the proper conditions are met, private owners of internationally mobile capital eliminate all repercussions of a basic disturbance on the foreign exchange market. The more these conditions are met, therefore, the smaller the need for governments to hold reserves with which to stabilize the exchange markets and, therefore, the closer to the origin will be the aggregate demand curve for reserves in Figure 1.

The attainment of these proper conditions involves the welfare losses which have been encountered in the analysis of the other determinants of the demand for reserves. The most important condition required is that interest rate differentials be set only for the attainment of external balance, which implies surrender of monetary policy as an instrument of full employment policies, except that forward exchange policy and Operation Twist succeed in establishing two different interest rates as was discussed above. The unavailability of monetary policy for domestic purposes frequently has adverse effects on welfare, since in practice fiscal policy in Western democracies has not been, and perhaps never can be, flexible enough to assure the maintenance of the socially optimal rate of employment in the way monetary policy is believed to be capable of doing. The welfare costs of foregone output, unemployment, and inflation have already been discussed.

The fact that stability of exchange rates benefits the short-term capital flow mechanism leads to an amendment of the preceding discussion of the welfare losses from the greater flexibility of exchange rates. In chapter 2 it had been argued that such flexibility has a dampening influence on the world level of trade and long-term capital flows. It is now necessary to add that greater flexibility also increases the need for international reserves and co-operation because it can lead to speculative short-term capital movements. In fact, theoretically, there can exist a certain quantity of speculative funds in the world and a pattern of speculative behaviour which causes the demand curve for reserves over a certain range to be sloped posi-ively, i.e. the opposite direction from that shown in Figure 1. However, it is a difficult problem to analyse whether the kind of speculative behaviour that has to be postulated in order to have a positively sloping demand curve can be found in the real world, especially in consideration of alternative institutions such as deep forward markets, active forward exchange policy, optimum currency areas, which may come into existence as a result of permanently greater exchange rate flexibility. The difference these institutional changes make for the argument, and the important problems of stabilizing and destabilizing exchange speculation will be discussed in chapter 6 below. For the remaining theoretical discussion of the welfare optimizing world monetary system, it will be assumed that the aggregate demand curve for international reserves is a decreasing function of the general propensity to make exchange rate adjustments.

Cost and Risk of Holding Reserves

In the model of the international monetary order considered thus far, it has been assumed that international reserves in the form of gold or universally acceptable national currencies yielded only the service of liquidity. However, a discussion of logically available alternative forms of organization must also consider the possibility that national currencies and new forms of reserves are not only liquid, but also bring benefits to its holders in the form of interest payments.

As was explained above, international reserves are acquired by national governments through the surrender of real resources (or claims on assets) by the running of balance-of-payments surpluses. If governments desire to maximize welfare in their country, they should push the acquisition of reserves to the point where the marginal social utility derived from the last unit held is just equal to the marginal social utility from alternative use of the resources. What are the components of the social utility from holding reserves? First, there is the income stream in the form of interest payments. Its capital value can be found by discounting the stream at an appropriate social discount rate. Second, there is the yield from liquidity. In the framework of the preceding analysis it is due to the fact that available reserves permit the government to intervene in the foreign exchange markets, maintain stable exchange rates, forego income and price adjustments, forego the surrender of national sovereignty, etc., with the resultant welfare gains discussed before. This 'welfare yield' from holding reserves in principle can be expressed as an annual rate of interest. It is reasonable to assume that this yield is a decreasing function of the quantity of reserves held on the grounds that the welfare gains from marginal increases in exchange rate, price and income stability and national sovereignty are probably smaller the greater the level of stability and sovereignty already achieved.

What determines the marginal social utility from the alternative use of the resources that have to be given up in exchange for the reserves through a balance-of-payments surplus? Since a balance-of-payments surplus is equivalent to social saving, in the sense that it represents either output produced but not consumed during the period or the net sale of real assets or claims on real assets formed earlier, it is best to consider the alternative cost as the foregone stream of income which the equivalent real resources would have yielded either in consumption or investment. The maximizing condition then states that the marginal social utility or productivity of a dollar's worth of output should be equal whether it is used for reserve accumulation, investment or consumption. Or, in other words, the discounted streams of income on marginal reserve accumulation or marginal investment should be equal to the marginal utility of consumption. For example, if reserves carry an interest rate just equal to the country's marginal productivity of capital, then the holding of reserves should be pushed until the marginal liquidity yield is zero, on the basis that if a country wishes to maximize the value of its national income, it should be indifferent between capital accumulation in the form of international reserves or real productive capital, as long as both forms yield equal streams of income.

In general, if a country is in equilibrium given the existing stock of and yield on reserves as well as the rate of return on real capital and marginal utility of consumption, then an increase in the interest rate paid on reserves creates a disequilibrium which can be corrected only by a lowering of the liquidity yield, which entails the net acquisition of reserves. Thus, the conclusion emerges that the demand for reserves is an increasing function of the interest rate paid to their holders.

In the real world yields on assets are never certain, and a large body of literature has developed which explains investment decisions under conditions of uncertainty. Some forms of reserves are subject to substantial degrees of income uncertainty. Gold, for example, has had a nominal value of $35 an ounce since the 1930s, but it has depreciated sharply in real purchasing power and many experts think that a future upward valuation may be expected sooner or later. National currencies used as reserves lose purchasing power whenever the countries issuing these currencies experience domestic inflation, whether or not they undertake a devaluation. Alternatively, price reductions and currency appreciation tend to raise the return from national currency holding. It may be reasonable to assume that national governments, like private investors, form expectations about future incomes from holding various forms of reserves, consider uncertainty a disutility that needs to be compensated for by income and generally adjust their portfolios in response to changes in these parameters.

There is some evidence that countries do in fact behave as the model suggests. Whenever a currency that serves as an international reserve vehicle is expected to undergo devaluation in the near future, the governments holding this currency tend to exchange it for gold or other 'safe' currencies. The United States and the United Kingdom have experienced some of these shifts in spite of great political pressures they have exerted in co-operative associations, trying to induce other countries to hold onto their sterling and dollar assets. Because of these political pressures, it is difficult to interpret the evidence on the interest rate elasticity of the demand for reserves, which had been found to be zero. In general, however, it is reasonable to conclude that, *ceteris paribus*, the greater the expected rates of return and the smaller the risk associated with assets serving as international reserves, the greater the demand for them.

World Price and Income Levels

In the preceding discussion it has been assumed implicitly that the world price level is constant. However, as is well known from monetary theory, the demand for money is a function of the price level and its rate of change. An analysis of these functional relationships in the context of the world monetary system will now be undertaken.

In Figure 2, representing a national market for foreign exchange in country A, the two axes have been denominated in units of foreign currency. Starting from the initial equilibrium situation shown in Figure 2, it is now assumed that all prices and the money supply in both countries A and B double exactly. Such an event leaves relative prices of commodities unchanged within and between the two countries, so that consumers' real demand for foreign products is unchanged (abstracting from the real balance effect). In terms of the graph, the assumed doubling of the world price level requires merely that the labels on the price axis be scaled upward by doubling the numbers. The elasticity of the schedules, however, is unaffected and any given real disturbance to equilibrium shifts schedules in the same proportion as when prices were at their old level.

However, at the higher price level any given deviation from equilibrium in real terms requires twice the nominal amount of foreign currency for successful stabilization than it did when all prices were lower by one half. Following the detailed analysis of chapter 2, this result of doubling prices can be seen to cause an outward shift of the world demand curve for reserves in Figure 1 to the point where, at any given level of exchange rate flexibility, the quantity of reserves demanded is exactly twice what it was before. In order to retain the intersection of the demand and supply curves at the level of exchange rate flexibility existing initially, the doubling of the world price level has to be accompanied by a doubling of the nominal value of reserves supplied. This analysis in terms of a doubling of the price level can be carried out for other equiproportional changes in all prices, and the general conclusion emerges that the demand for international reserves is a function of the world price level, more specifically that the elasticity of demand with respect to prices is unity.[5]

In the context of a generally inflationary world economy where expected future price changes are important, the rate of increase in the demand for international reserves is a decreasing function of the rate of increase in the price level, though the precise functional relationship is quite complex and can be discussed here only sketchily. In general there are two opposing forces at work simultaneously. First, there is the effect discussed in the preceding paragraph, namely that given real disturbances require larger nominal balances the higher the general price level. Offsetting this demand is the second effect that inflation is a tax on money balances which lowers the yield of holding reserves. The precise nature of this effect will be dis-

5. The neo-classical synthesis in economics which had taken place during the 1950s produced a thorough understanding of the conditions necessary to make money a veil, and the price elasticity of the demand for money unity in comparative static equilibrium analysis. Many of the finer points of this analysis, such as the real-balance effect, the need for doubling of the prices of all fixed income bearing securities, the absence of money illusion, etc., have been left out of the preceding discussion in order to keep it simple and short. It is clear, however, that these conditions also have to be fulfilled in connexion with the international monetary analysis if the demand for reserves is to be of unitary price elasticity.

cussed at greater length in chapter 8, where it will be seen that it depends on the level of interest paid on reserves, the responsiveness of the rates to inflationary trends, on the international distribution of the price increases, and on the readiness of countries to make exchange rate adjustments. The more institutional arrangements succeed in protecting the real value of reserve balances against inflation, the greater will be the demand for reserves at any given rate of price increases.

The position of the demand curve for reserves in Figure 1 is also influenced by the level of real income in the world. Assuming that prices remain constant, growth in real income in both countries A and B tends to shift outward the demand and supply schedules for foreign exchange in Figure 2. If countries grow at unequal rates then in the framework of the concepts developed in connexion with Figure 2, the country with the greater rate of growth will find its demand curve for foreign exchange shift outward more rapidly than the supply curve for foreign exchange (assuming equal marginal propensities to import for both countries). The resultant deficit has to be financed by the use of reserves or eliminated by some other policies in the manner discussed above. In general it holds true that the greater the divergence in the growth rates of countries over any finite time period the greater, *ceteris paribus*, will be the world demand for international reserves.

In a situation where growth rates and marginal propensities to import are equal in both countries the demand and supply curves for foreign exchange shift equiproportionately, and deficits do not appear as a result of the growth itself. In spite of this absence of deficits, however, real growth of world output leads to an increased demand for reserves for three reasons. First, basic disturbances to equilibrium, such as changes in taste or technology, typically have an effect that is proportional to the given level of output. For example, a certain technical innovation that makes country A's automobiles more attractive to residents of country B, can most reasonably be assumed to cause a switch of purchases equal to say, 10 per cent of automobiles bought during a given period. Thus, if the level of automobile sales is 1000 a 10 per cent shift involves 100 automobiles, whereas the shift is equal to 150 if the level of production is at 1500. Thus, the quantity of reserves required to compensate for the destabilizing effect of a given technical disturbance is greater the higher the level of income.

Second, the size of national incomes determines the welfare cost of using domestic price and income adjustments for the sake of exchange rate stability. It has been argued earlier that in the modern world there exists a link between rates of change in the price level and the rate of unemployment. From this argument it follows that domestic adjustment to an external equilibrium may require increasing the rate of unemployment by, say, one percentage point. Such a reduction in employment causes a loss of output in real terms that is greater the greater the basic level of productive capacity.

Third, the higher level of income, *ceteris paribus*, tends to lower the marginal utility of income. Therefore, a given loss of output represents a lower loss in total welfare the greater the level of output. This factor tends to lower the demand for reserves as world income increases.

In general, the first two factors tend to shift outward the demand curve for reserves as world income goes up while the third factor tends to operate in the opposite direction. As a result of the existence of these forces operating in opposite directions, *a priori* reasoning does not permit any statements about the income elasticity of the demand for reserves, i.e. whether at the same level of exchange rate flexibility, co-operation, etc., a proportional increase in income increases or decreases the demand for reserves in the same, larger, or smaller proportion. The exact functional relationship has to be determined empirically. Unfortunately, there exists a scarcity of empirical studies applicable to this problem.

The previous discussion of the determinants of the

demand for reserves derived a theoretical condition concerning the degree of exchange rate flexibility, co-operation, domestic adjustments, etc., which tends to maximize world welfare. Theoretically, there exists such a condition also for the rate of growth in real world income (and the accompanying price changes via the Phillips curve). A given outward shift of the demand curve may require increased exchange rate flexibility, co-operation, supplies of reserves or domestic adjustments, each of which entail welfare losses in the manner analysed above, and it is conceivable though highly unlikely that these losses would outweigh the gains made through increased income, and optimality demands that income be reduced. Formally, the maximizing condition states that the welfare loss from a marginal reduction in income should just be equal to the loss resulting from a marginal use of greater exchange rate flexibility, etc.

In practice it is very difficult to conceive that a reduction in real income (or the rate of increase in real income) would ever be required for the sake of welfare maximization. Income affects human well-being directly; its maintenance or growth is the very end of economic activity, while all of the other factors influencing the demand for reserves affect welfare more or less indirectly and, in comparison, by a small amount. Because of this empirical significance of income for welfare, it can be argued that the world's international payments mechanism should be designed so that the desired growth in world real income be realized efficiently, and at the minimum loss of welfare from the other sources discussed in the last two chapters.

National Demand for Reserves

The preceding theoretical considerations have been aimed at the derivation of world welfare maximizing demand and supply schedules for international reserves. Underlying the demand schedule are individual country demand curves, and the concepts of the propensity to make exchange rate, income and other adjustments for the world as a whole are built upon individual countries' willingness to make these adjustments under the appropriate circumstances. In the remaining part of this chapter an attempt will be made to analyse a few of the factors determining *national* differences in the demand for international reserves and the willingness to make balance-of-payments adjustments of various types.

At the outset it has to be emphasized that the demand for reserves and the need to make adjustments by all countries are strongly interdependent. In a world consisting of two countries it is most obvious that if one runs a balance-of-payments surplus and makes no adjustments to curb it, the second country has to carry all of the adjustment burden, and in general, the more adjustments are undertaken by the one the fewer have to be made by the other. Implicit in the general conditions of world welfare maximizing propensities to make exchange rate and other adjustments is a unique international distribution of these adjustment burdens and therefore a unique pattern of behaviour and demand for international reserves by each country.

This uniqueness, however, does not imply equality of behaviour and demand for reserves by individual countries faced with identical disequilibria. There are at least eight important factors entering into the determination of these national differences.

First, the size of the marginal propensity to import determines how big a country's domestic real income changes have to be if it chooses to correct a balance-of-payments deficit in this manner. For example, if the marginal propensity to import is 0·1, then the elimination of a $1 million deficit requires an income reduction of $10 million whereas the same deficit requires an income reduction of only $2 million if the marginal propensity to import is 0·5. Thus, the cost of running out of reserves and having to use income adjustments to correct a given balance-of-payments deficit is greater the smaller the marginal propensity to import. Therefore, national demand for reserves is a decreasing function of the marginal propensity to import.

Second, the greater a country's foreign trade sector the more significant are the effects of a given real disturbance to foreign demand or supply. For example, if 10 per cent of the normal foreign customers of a country's automobiles don't like the new styles and switch to another country's output, the total dollar value of the decrease in exports is greater the greater the normal level of automobile exports that is the base to which the 10 per cent figure has to be applied. For this reason the absolute level of the national demand for reserves is an increasing function of the absolute size of the foreign trade sector.

Third, the greater the probability and magnitude of cyclical and random fluctuations in the demand for or supply of a country's export and import commodities the greater are the fluctuations in the balance of payments. For example, agricultural products typically are subject to seasonal and random fluctuations of supply and prices. Some manufactured products suffer more than others from cyclical instabilities of sales due to the high income elasticity of the demand for them. Still other manufactured products are subject to frequent technological and stylistic changes, which cause demand to be unstable. How widely and for what length of time a given country's trade balance tends to be imbalanced depends therefore on the relevant characteristics of the products entering its foreign trade. In general, the more unstable the demand for or supply of a country's commodities traded abroad, the greater that country's demand for reserves.

Fourth, as a corollary to the preceding condition the smaller the correlation of demand and supply fluctuations of individual commodities the more stable the average demand and supply and the smaller the demand for reserves. Generally, the greater the number of different products in a country's foreign trade the greater is the probability that given instabilities in demand or supply for individual products tend to offset each other, and therefore the greater tends to be the over-all stability of the trade balance and the smaller the demand for reserves.

Fifth, the preceding four points concerning the size, demand elasticity and structural characteristics of individual countries' foreign trade have their nearly identical counterparts in the foreign capital section of the balance of payments. Thus, the larger a country's absolute size of foreign investments at home or abroad, the greater the interest sensitivity and cyclical instability of various types of capital flows, and the smaller the diversity of the types of capital, the greater therefore is the instability of that country's capital account balance and, *ceteris paribus*, its demand for international reserves.

Sixth, the flexibility of domestic wages and prices and the general mobility of resources in a country facilitate the economy's adjustment to external disturbances. Therefore, the greater this flexibility and mobility, the shorter is the duration of a given cyclical or random deficit in the balance of trade or capital flows and the smaller a country's demand for reserves.

Seventh, the *per capita* income and wealth of nations tends to influence their demand for reserves in two distinct ways. First, a high income, wealthy country can afford more readily to keep a share of its national wealth in foreign reserves because the social opportunity cost of these resources tends to be lower than it is in countries with lower income and wealth *per capita* due to the operation of the principle of decreasing marginal utility of income. Second, the greater the wealth holdings in a country the greater tends to be the stock of financial claims which can readily be shifted abroad for speculative purposes, or to take advantage of higher interest rates. For both of these reasons the demand for international reserves is an increasing function of nations' *per capita* income and wealth.

Eighth, countries, like individuals, have different attitudes towards risk, which enter the determination of the demand for reserves through the fact that future balance-of-payments disequilibria are uncertain. In the pure case of such uncertainty developed in the random walk model above, it is possible to derive a probability distribution of cumulative reserve losses of a given size at a given time in the future. However, whether a country at any moment in time wishes to be protected against the loss of all reserves over a time horizon of 5, 10 or 100 years, with the probability of 0·01, 0·1 or 0·9 depends on its attitudes towards the risk. While the cost of running out of reserves and the opportunity cost of holding them enter into the determination of this attitude, the tastes of individual countries are important determinants as well. A given set of probable future reserve losses, cost of holding reserves, and cost of making adjustments may make one country's leaders to regard a certain level of reserves adequate, while another country's leaders under the identical circumstances may consider that same level of reserves to be perfectly inadequate. The element of taste entering this determination of the optimum level of reserves is the same which makes one salesman travelling in a motor car carry $100 as a precautionary reserve against the breakdown of his automobile in a strange town and the probability of missing an important sales meeting, while another salesman under the same circumstances carries $200. In general, the greater a country's dislike for the risk of being caught short of reserves and having to face exchange rate and domestic adjustments, the greater will be a country's demand for reserves.

In practice it has been very difficult to establish empirically these various factors' relative importance in determining intercountry differences in reserve holdings. The main reasons for this difficulty are both theoretical and statistical. The theoretical model of a world where countries behave to maximize *world* welfare is not realistic. Countries tend to try to maximize their own welfare and the adjustment burdens typically tend to be put on deficit countries. In recent decades this practice has resulted in the imposition of restrictions on trade and capital flows, and exchange rate adjustments which have distorted both the size of reserve holdings as well as the levels and composition of trade and capital flows. Consequently, *ex post* data on reserve holdings and levels of trade and capital flows fail to reflect the patterns of national behaviour which would have resulted from an unimpeded operation of the theoretical principles of behaviour just discussed. These distortions are aggravated by the existence of any shortages or excesses in the supply of international reserves from their welfare maximizing level.

Statistically the problem with measurement has been the great degree of multi-collinearity among the determinants of the demand for reserves. Empirically it turns out that countries with large absolute foreign trade sectors also have high *per capita* incomes, widely diversified export and import trade, large foreign capital stocks and flows, and relatively flexible and adjustable domestic economies. For this reason it is difficult to separate out statistically the relative importance of each of these factors independently.

One widely used practical and rather unsophisticated measure of the demand for reserves by individual countries and in the aggregate has been the ratio of reserves to international trade. The preceding analysis of this chapter has shown the inadequacy of this measure from a theoretical point of view. However, because there exists this great degree of correlation among the determinants of the demand for reserves, this measure can serve as a useful surrogate for these other determinants in the short-run, especially in combination with other information on the adjustment and restrictive policies imposed by deficit and surplus countries. In the long run, however, and for the sake of logical rigour, the demand for reserves and tests of supply adequacy have to consider all of the theoretical determinants.

4 The Adequacy of a World Monetary Order and Types of Reform

This chapter puts to use the analytical model of world monetary organization presented in the preceding two chapters by developing, first, a conceptual framework for examining the adequacy of an existing monetary order and second, a simple scheme for the classification of recent proposals for world monetary reform.

Measures of Adequacy

It appears to be very difficult to reach a consensus among economists, monetary technicians, bankers and politicians about the adequacy of an existing monetary order and the sources of any of the system's shortcomings. The reasons for this lack of agreement are numerous.

First, there is the traditional reluctance of central bankers to change the *status quo*. These men carry heavy burdens of responsibility for the proper functioning of national monetary systems, the failure of which has vast implications for the welfare of their countries. Therefore, these men are reluctant to experiment with ideas for reform thought out by academicians in their ivory towers, eager to claim for themselves a place in intellectual history, but essentially unable to bear the responsibility in any meaningful sense for the possibly harmful consequences of their ideas. Because of this vested interest in the *status quo* and in the absence of risky experimentation, central bankers have a tendency to argue for the merits of the existing system and minimize its shortcomings.

Second, as was discussed in chapter 1, any existing monetary order benefits nations in relatively different degrees, reflecting the structure of military and economic power at the time of the order's inception. Therefore, certain countries have a vested interest in preserving the system which, at least in theory, was designed to give them greater prestige, power or resources.

Third, agreement over the nature of the deficiencies of an existing system very often implies agreement over the general direction of future changes. But since a changed monetary order brings benefits to countries in different relative magnitudes than before, some countries are reluctant to cast their vote for a certain diagnosis for fear that it commits them to the acceptance of a remedy yielding fewer benefits than they believe to be deserving, given the existing distribution of national, economic and military power.

Fourth, even among technicians and economists, who through their training and positions of political independence can abstract from the first three sources of disagreement, there is often an inability to agree over the existence and nature of deficiencies in the world monetary order. This lack of agreement is due to the complexity of the technical issues involved, a failure to spell out assumptions about the nature of the real world and to distinguish value judgements from empirical economic estimates measurable, at least, in principle.

The measure for the adequacy of a world monetary system about to be developed serves to narrow the areas of disagreement among technicians and economists by reducing the complexity of the basic problem. The framework for achieving this result already has been laid in the preceding chapters and in the remaining part of this chapter it will be directed explicitly at the construction of the test.

As a first task it is necessary to clarify the nature of the disturbances to national payments equilibria which are assumed to give rise to the need for an international monetary mechanism. National balance of payments tend to get out of order from time to time because of a variety of reasons such as technical changes altering the cost of production, relative prices of factors and final products; changes in the tastes of consumers, causing different patterns of expenditures at given relative prices of consumer goods; differing rates of national economic growth and price changes due either to different rates of population growth, rates of capital formation and judgements about the evils of inflation by individual countries, or due to the inability to control domestic economic events, either because of political considerations or because of technical inadequacies; national catastrophes, such as failure of harvests, wars, epidemics or property destruction by earthquakes, fire, flood or insurrection, which temporarily reduce countries' ability to produce at normal levels and force them to import more and export less in order to maintain their populations at a standard of living reasonably close to the one sustainable under normal conditions.

These sources of disturbance must be taken as given and considered to be the world, imperfect as it is, to which the human institution of world monetary order must be adapted. By making this assumption, the following analysis is protected against the argument that a given international monetary system would be adequate if only there were fewer natural catastrophes and wars or there was greater technological and cyclical stability, etc. The reason for the selection of the specific set of external disturbances is the empirical judgement that some of these conditions giving rise to disequilibria simply cannot be changed, such as natural catastrophes, or that interference with them has such obvious and large negative effects on welfare that the adaptation of the monetary order will always be more efficient, as, for example, in the case of technological change. Technological change is essential for economic growth and preventing it from taking place for the sake of stability in international payments would be like killing the goose that lays the golden eggs.

The analysis of the world monetary mechanism in the

preceding chapters focused on the demand for and supply of international reserves. It is in the nature of all market analysis that the intersection of the demand and supply schedules *ex post*, always represents an 'equilibrium', a combination of quantity and price at which the market was cleared. In the case of international reserves, represented by Figure 1 and the analysis surrounding it, it is also true that *ex post* the world is always in 'equilibrium' in the sense that the demand for reserves equals the available supply. The fact is almost a truism, yet it is the source of some difficulties in judging the adequacy of a world monetary order. The gold exchange standard of the post Second World War era resulted in no 'obvious' dis-equilibria. There were no market disorders typically associated with commodities in short supply and at fixed disequilibrium prices, there were no general reserve short-ages publicized by any governments. The reason for this absence of any obvious disequilibria is that countries always acted so that, in fact, the sum of reserves demanded was equal to the available supply.

However, it is these latter actions by the governments, which must be considered as evidence in tests of the adequacy of a monetary system. The nature of these governmental policies has already been discussed, and it was discovered that there are 'ideal' levels of national willingness to adopt income and price changes, to accept exchange rate variations, to engage in non-price restric-tions of international trade, to perfect private short-term capital mobility, to co-operate and co-ordinate economic policies internationally, and that there is an 'ideal' level of international reserves which would maximize world wel-fare, given available resources, basic tastes, technical and cultural conditions in existence. These policy tools to-gether represent an interdependent system which works efficiently when the loss in welfare associated with the marginal increase in the use of any one variable is just equal to the losses associated with the marginal use of each of the others. For example, the system is efficient if a marginal increase in countries' readiness to use exchange rate variations causes reduced world output and welfare of a given size, because the increased price uncertainty represents a cost of doing business and lowers the level of international specialization and the movement of factors of production. This given size of welfare loss should just be equal to the one encountered when through a marginal increase in international co-operation countries and individuals have to surrender some of their right to be different and enjoy their characteristic cultural heritage. The character and the source of welfare losses from the marginal increase in the use of the other policies affecting the demand for reserves were analysed in chapters 2 and 3 above.

With all policy instruments set at these optimizing levels, the positions of the demand and supply curves are thus given, and along with them is given a unique point in the quantity of reserves and flexibility of exchange rates space of Figure 1 at which world welfare is maximized through optimum levels of international trade and working of adjustments.[1] In discussions of the adequacy or short-comings of an existing international monetary system it is necessary, therefore, to seek agreement, first, on whether the world is at this point of optimality and second, if it is not, the use of which policy instruments is responsible for this deviation from optimality.

Unfortunately, economics is not able to provide scientific answers to these questions because the science of measure-

1. This concept of a world welfare maximizing supply and demand for international reserves is closely related to the concept of a 'full employment budget surplus' recently developed by the United States Council of Economic Advisors during the chairmanship of Walter Heller. It indicates what would be the government's budget surplus if the economy operated at full employment without the fiscal constraint represented by the existing tax structure. Sir Roy Harrod developed a similar concept, the full-growth balance of payments, as a measure of Britain's payments balance that would exist if the external constraint on British economic growth policies were absent. See Harrod (1967). By analogy, the demand for reserves discussed here would result if the constraints on the level of international trade through international reserve availability were at its 'ideal' level in the sense discussed in the text.

ment in economics has not progressed far enough and probably never will, since the measurement involved requires interpersonal comparisons of utility. In place of such measurement the world must do with the judgements of experts. These judgements during the period 1958–67 were most often that the current gold exchange standard caused the world to operate its international economic relations at less than optimum levels. The majority of experts considered the prime manifestations of this short-coming to have been in the growth of national restrictions on international trade and the frequent use of domestic price and income adjustments by many countries, but especially by some of the major industrial countries. In the framework of the analysis surrounding Figure 1, such a diagnosis is equivalent to saying that if countries had operated at a desirable level of domestic restrictions and income changes, an upward shift of the demand curve would have taken place and resulted in the appearance of an *ex ante* excess demand for reserves at the existing level of supply and at the prevailing level of exchange rate flexibility. Because of this *ex ante* shortage countries had to engage in these undesirable practices, shifted down the demand curve and created an *ex post* equality of demand and supply.

While this analysis leads to the diagnosis that has received the greatest publicity, namely that there was a shortage of international reserves, the preceding analysis of chapters 2 and 3 suggests that this is only one of several logical alternative interpretations of the basic difficulties. For example, the *ex ante* excess demand for reserves can also be interpreted as being due to an unwarranted lack of willingness by many countries to co-operate inter-nationally or to engage in exchange rate adjustments. These kinds of interpretations have in fact been advanced by several of the experts and have led them to recommend a host of proposals for reform closely related to their diagnosis of the system's basic ills.

Survey of Reform Proposals

The following discussion will state in very simplified terms
the basic arguments used by the proponents of the various
plans for reform, using as much as possible the analytical
framework developed earlier in this book. All of the
proponents of the individual plans have made the empirical judgement that the adoption of their proposals
would lead to an improvement of world welfare. The
validity of these judgements will not be examined here
but in the chapters of Part Two where the workings of
the prototypes of world monetary order are analysed at
length. The remaining part of this chapter contains merely
an uncritical statement of the various positions and an
analysis of the way in which they fit into the general
theoretical construct developed above.

Flexible Exchange Rates

James Meade's position is representative of the view that
greater flexibility of exchange rates would permit countries
to maintain optimum levels of restrictions and other
policies and yet manage with the quantity and nature of
international reserves existing in the world. In the general
analytical framework developed earlier, this argument is
equivalent to saying that countries should use their
income, trade restrictions and other policies influencing
the demand for reserves in such ways as to maximize world
welfare, which under present conditions presumably would
shift the demand curve upward and to the right. They
should then be prepared to accept whatever exchange
rate flexibility is necessary to assure both *ex ante* and
ex post equality of demand and supply of reserves. A free
market for reserves, be they gold or national currencies,
would result in the creation of a stock of reserves sufficient
so that countries could operate the policy instruments at a
world welfare maximizing level.

Milton Friedman is representative of the view that

countries should denounce *all* official responsibilities for the maintenance of exchange rates and should leave them to fluctuate freely. Such a policy would immediately cause the demand for reserves to be zero and would permit nations to forego the use of the policies they had developed to overcome their balance-of-payments problems. Thus, income and price changes, restrictions on trade, international co-operation, etc., could be abandoned or set at levels optimizing welfare within given other technical and political constraints.

It is clear that implicit in both of these recommendations is the empirical judgement that greater or perfect flexibility of exchange rates would have negative welfare effects smaller than those resulting from greater exchange rate stability with all the undesirable policies necessary to maintain them.

Gold Standard

Jacques Rueff and Michael Heilperin are the best-known exponents of the view that the existing system's ills should be corrected by re-introduction of the true gold standard. The essential ingredients of such a reform are twofold. First, it entails an increase in the price of gold, which is equivalent to an outward shift of the supply schedule for international reserves in Figure 1. Second, it requires that national governments submit their domestic policies to the discipline of the balance of payments, allowing income and price inflation when it is in surplus and deflation when it is in deficit. As a result of this willingness to adjust domestic prices and incomes, the demand curve for reserves is shifted downward permitting perfect exchange rate stability at the level of available reserves. The theoretical analysis of a world welfare maximizing order suggests that this supply of reserves be set at a level where the other balance-of-payments policies can be used to the optimum degree in the sense developed above.

Increased Private Capital Mobility

James Ingram has argued that as a result of the two world wars and the economic nationalism of the twentieth century, private short-term capital mobility has been impaired through government rules and regulations. As a result, the world has failed to take advantage of the great cushioning effect of these flows which, as was argued in chapter 2, are essentially a substitute for official stabilization in the foreign exchange markets. As such, greater private short-term capital mobility shifts downward the schedule of demand for reserves and ideally would do so to the extent that existing supplies are sufficient to assure the optimal use of exchange rate variations, income adjustments, etc. The discussion of the disturbing effect of short-term capital flows in a world where monetary policy is used to stabilize domestic income and prices, suggests that the effectiveness of this reform depends on countries' willingness to surrender monetary policy as a tool of domestic policy making, or to subject themselves to more international co-operation with the concomitant loss of national sovereignty.

Improved Gold Exchange Standard

The best known proponents of the following kind of reasoning have been Henry Wallich, Edward Bernstein, Xenophon Zolotas and Robert Roosa as well as the officials of the International Monetary Fund and the central bankers of the Western world. These men have argued essentially that the existing international monetary order is adequate to meet the world's need for the efficient working of its international payments as long as some minor institutional changes are undertaken. One of these changes involves greater international co-operation at the highest levels of government, which reduces the incidence of inconsistent national monetary and fiscal policies. It would also lead to agreements on mutual assistance and the availability of stand-by credits. As was argued in chapter 2, such co-operation leads to a downward shift of the demand curve. Another change would involve granting of gold guarantees on national currencies held by governments as reserves, thus reducing the risk of holding them and increasing the quantity of currencies available as official reserve vehicles. Still other institutional changes envisage that the reserves, created through the International Monetary Fund, be increased and generally made available more readily.

Presumably, these institutional innovations could be pushed to the point where the available reserves are adequate to permit governments to keep direct controls, exchange rate variations, etc., at levels appropriate for the maximization of world welfare.

Centrally Created Reserves

Proposals for reform of the international monetary order through the creation of an institution that expands the supply of reserves through fiat, are associated with the names of John Maynard Keynes, Robert Triffin, Maxwell Stamp, Robert Roosa and Edward Bernstein in their later writings, the Group of Ten, and others.

Some of the proposals advanced by these men are different in institutional details of little real importance. Others differ in essentials, such as the rate of growth in reserves, the acceptability of these reserves, the distribution of the resources potentially accruing to the issuing institution, the role of interest payments in the scheme, the treatment of gold, etc. However, in spite of these differences there exists the overwhelmingly important similarity, that these plans aim at an increase in the supply of reserves at such a rate that all national policies can be kept at the welfare maximizing levels. As was argued in chapter 2, however, the use of these reserves itself leads to potential welfare losses when certain countries find themselves obliged to accept such fiat money in return for real resources transferred to deficit countries. The frequency and insistency with which such events are likely to take place depends, *ceteris paribus*, on the size of the reserve pool created. Moreover, countries may prefer to be on different positions on their national Phillips curves. Yet, the rate of international reserve creation influences the overall world trade-off between inflation and unemployment, imposing welfare losses on countries desiring different world price level charges and rates of unemployment than those generated by the centrally created reserves. In the absence of any scientifically valid measurements of these losses, it has proved to be very difficult to agree on an optimal level or rate of increase of the supply of reserves.

Part Two   The Theory and History of Organizational Prototypes

In the first part of this text the characteristics of a welfare maximizing international monetary order were analysed from a mostly theoretical point of view. In the present part four prototypes of world monetary organization that have actually existed at one time, or that have been recommended for institution in the future, are examined with a special view towards assessment of their past and potential future performance merits. These prototypes are the gold standard, flexible exchange rates, the gold exchange standard and the central creation of international reserves.

The discussion of each of these forms of organization consists of three parts. The first part contains a basic theoretical model highlighting the essential operating features and real effects of the prototype. The second part summarizes its actual historic development and performance, emphasizing the modifications of the basic model undertaken in the real world, and analysing its success in permitting economic growth and stability. The third part presents an analysis of the sources of welfare losses required to make the theoretical prototype work under current conditions, using, whenever possible, the theoretical tools of analysis developed in Part One.

5 The Gold Standard

The Basic Model

The theoretical blueprint of the basic classical gold standard is based on assumptions about the real world that are normally made in the teaching of classical economic theory and general equilibrium analysis: the economy operates under conditions of perfect competition, prices and wages are perfectly flexible, there is always full employment of resources, money is held only for transaction purposes, and the institutional arrangements determining this transaction demand change only slowly. In addition, it is convenient to assume that the money supply consists entirely of gold, which is also acceptable in the settlement of debts between nations. For heuristic reasons the following discussion proceeds in terms of a two-country world, where there are neither technical change nor economic growth and where there are no autonomous capital movements between the two countries.

In an economy where these basic conditions are met the quantity theory of money holds. This theory can best be explained by presentation of the basic and well-known identity: $M \times V \equiv P \times Q$, where M is the quantity of money, V is the transactions velocity of money (i.e. how often a unit of money is spent over a given time period, a fact determined by the economy's institutions regarding patterns of payments and receipts), P is an index of all prices in the economy (i.e. the price level) and Q is an index of the volume of physical transactions resulting from a given full employment level of national output. Alternative specifications of this identity consider Q to be the physical volume of goods and services produced over a given time period. With this specification of Q, V is defined as the income velocity of money. Either definition of Q and V is legitimate and no substantive changes in the conclusions of the basic analysis follow from the adoption of one or the other definition. Under both systems, given the indices of Q and P and the nomincal value of M, V is derived by simple division, i.e. $V \equiv PQ/M$.

The basic identity of the equation $MV \equiv PQ$, can be made into an analytically useful theory by the assumption that V is unalterably fixed in the short run and that P adjusts passively to exogenous changes in M or Q. According to this theory it follows that if a government tries to increase the quantity of gold circulating in its country through the imposition of appropriate laws and regulations, then the result of such efforts will be an increase in P proportional to the increase in M, since Q is given at its full employment level and V is constant. Alternatively, with M unchanged, the autonomous decrease of Q resulting from a poor harvest, flood or war devastation also results in an increase in P proportional to the decrease in Q.

The preceding example of a government induced increase in M is of great historical interest, since it describes the activities of the mercantilist governments of the seventeenth and eighteenth centuries, and stimulated David Hume to present a well articulated version of the quantity theory of money which he then applied to the demonstration of the absurdity of these mercantilist policies. As the increase in circulating money raised the price level, the country's balance of trade would turn to a deficit requiring settlement in gold and continuing until the domestic money supply had returned to its previous level, thus eliminating all of the gold gains the mercantilist policies had achieved through the imposition of unpopular and socially costly restrictions on international economic relations.

The same quantity theory model of the economy was

later used to analyse more formally the process of international adjustments under the gold standard. Under classical assumptions about the real world the most prominent sources of disturbance to international equilibrium were those hypothesized in the preceding examples, namely natural or man-made catastrophes which reduced the physical quantity of a nation's output during a given period of time. As had already been argued, the result of such catastrophes is an increase in the domestic price level, which induces foreigners to reduce their purchases and domestic residents to increase their purchases abroad, leading to a payments deficit and an outflow of gold. As a result of the reduced stock of money in the economy, the price level falls and the size of the deficit in the following period is reduced. With the national output remaining at its catastrophe-reduced level, the deficit, gold losses and price reductions continue in subsequent periods until prices reach a level where the payments imbalance is zero. The attainment of this equilibrium is aided if the gold transfers cause an increased money supply and rise in the price level in the rest of the world, thus helping to offset some of the initial price disadvantage of the country with the basic difficulties. The adjustment mechanism ultimately produces the condition where at the temporarily lowered level of Q, the quantity of M is just sufficient to keep the economy at the price level P which given V, and the price level in the rest of the world, results in balanced external payments.

After the country with the original disequilibrium restores its national output to the normal level, its existing price level falls further still, as it must if the basic identity $MV \equiv PQ$ is to hold and M and V are given. The lower price level causes the appearance of a trade surplus, an increase in M and a rise in prices. This process of gaining gold and raising the price level continues until the old, pre-catastrophe level of the money supply and prices are reached in both the original deficit country and the rest of the world and international payments are balanced.

This basic model is applicable in modified form to the explanation of adjustments to causes of payments disequilibria other than natural catastrophes, such as changes in taste and technology, shifts of capital, domestic inflation due to excess spending and others. In all of these cases resultant deficits are cured by domestic price reductions, which the gold losses bring about automatically in the manner described. However, as for the ultimate adjustments, the present cases differ from those of natural catastrophes in that the original national incomes, prices and gold stocks may not be re-established in the new equilibrium. For example, as a result of a change in tastes, a country may find its output valued lower by the rest of the world, the terms of trade moved adversely and the value of national income lowered, thus requiring a lower stock of gold for normal transactions.

In general, the basic mechanism for the international adjustment of national payments imbalances under the gold standard has several outstanding advantages. First, there is the expectation of stable long run prices between all countries. Price levels between countries may diverge occasionally and temporarily, but such episodes are likely to be no more intense or lengthy than price divergences between the regions of a major country, each of which are also subject to natural catastrophes. As was argued before, such stability of prices and values between nations encourages the development of international trade and the free flow of capital. From this point of view the whole world becomes one 'country' with the only essential differences that there are national governments, with the right to tax and wage wars and restrict the free movement of people. Otherwise, the allocation of resources in the world as a whole tends to be efficient as it is within a country.

Second, implicit in the analysis of the gold standard's financial mechanism is a beneficial flow of real resources. When a country finds its output temporarily reduced by one event or another, its population, *ceteris paribus*, would have to reduce its standard of living drastically, and by the full amount of the lost output during the period when the harvest failed or productive resources have been destroyed, if it did not have the option to use some of its circulating gold to purchase goods from foreigners and thus decrease the severity of the imposed income reduction for the moment. Ultimately the country's population has to absorb the consequences of the original calamity through a reduced standard of living, but under the gold standard it can do so over a longer period of time and with smaller sacrifices per time period than it would have to without the gold standard.[1] Since this benefit is available to all nations on the gold standard, this organization of the international payments system amounts to an efficient and equitable system of insurance against natural catastrophes and mutual assistance for the world as a whole.

Third, the gold standard as described in the basic model functions without any government intervention. This is a great advantage in the eyes of people who believe that the efficient allocation of resources is such a complex problem, that no human being can ever have all of the relevant information and necessary foresight to devise policies that can assure that the economy operates efficiently. In addition, such government intervention in the economic sphere represents a reduction in economic liberty, and in the long run, personal freedom in a pluralistic society cannot exist without liberty in the sphere of economics. From this point of view it is a great advantage that the gold standard operates without economic policies made by governments, and thus permits restriction of government activity to the provision of national defence,

1. This argument fails to spell out the alternative system replacing the gold standard. Such a discussion would complicate the present analysis unduly, but it is worth pointing out as a general methodological problem that the merits of all institutional innovations need to be compared with the next best institutional alternative, just as the cost of reserves used in producing a certain product is measured in economics in terms of 'opportunity costs', or what they would have yielded in their next best alternative employment·

other genuinely public goods, and the maintenance of domestic law and order.

The Model and the Real World

An important set of theoretical modifications of the gold standard model was undertaken in response to empirical findings. Professor Taussig at Harvard and some of his students had examined statistics of price and gold movements during periods when the gold standard was in actual operation. They discovered that even some of the severest disruptions of balance-of-payments equilibria were accompanied by actual gold movements of such minor size that they had to be considered incapable of explaining the process of adjustment predicted by the basic classical model.

The theoretical modifications of the basic gold standard model that developed in response to these findings fall into three distinct groups. First, the model was adapted to account explicitly for private short-term capital movements. Thus, if, as in the framework of the previous analysis, the cause of the international disturbance is assumed to be the failure of a harvest, the deficit causes prices to rise and gold to be exported in the manner described before. The additional element of the analysis is, however, that farmers try to borrow funds to tide them over the period of calamity. Since this demand represents a net addition to the equilibrium quantity of loans demanded and supplied at the existing interest rate, the market rate of interest goes up. In real terms, because of the destruction of resources in the deficit country the marginal productivity of capital is temporarily raised.

As a result of this rise in the interest rate, private short-term capital is attracted into the deficit country. These capital imports are equivalent to the export of goods and services, in fact they *are* the export of claims on assets, enabling the deficit country to increase its imports of food products above the levels permitted by its own current exports of goods and services alone. The resultant increase in food supplies keeps down the rise in prices and the loss of gold. The extent to which this process is effective depends on the institutionally determined interest elasticity of private short-term funds. If the elasticity is very great, a very small rise in the interest rate causes sufficient capital inflows to prevent any further price increases and gold losses. At lower elasticities the benefits are correspondingly smaller.

In real terms these capital imports amount to the mortgaging of national assets other than gold, in return for the temporary loan of resources needed to overcome the effects of the bad harvest. Mortgaging of these assets other than money has the advantage of limiting the extent to which the price level has to rise initially and fall in the subsequent period of adjustment.

In the model with short-term capital flows the assets are repurchased from foreigners when, upon the restoration of the crop to its normal level, the farmers begin to repay their loans and interest rates fall. Consequently, foreigners divest themselves of their holdings, acquire gold and repatriate it. As a result of this gold transfer prices fall in the country that had the poor harvest and rise in the other, causing the appearance of a trade surplus for the former and the transfer of the real resources borrowed originally.

In the real world during the gold standard, private short-term capital was rather interest-elastic because of the confidence investors had in the stability of exchange rates and national price levels. However, as will be discussed below, the private short-term capital movements under the gold standard were dominated by events in London, and worked primarily to the benefit of the United Kingdom, rather than of all countries as the theoretical model suggests.

The second modification of the basic classical model, represents an explanation of the small actual gold movements discovered by Taussig which is essentially a logical rival to the explanation involving capital movements. This modification received a complete and thorough explanation through the systematic development of Keynesian economics. In this system of analysis the classical model of the economy is made more realistic by the explicit recognition of the downward rigidity of real wages and prices.

In the Keynesian model exogeneously caused decreases in aggregate demand such as following a poor harvest have further repercussions. Suppliers of farmers find their sales decreased since the farmers do not have the purchasing power to buy the normal quantity of farm inputs and consumer products. Other businessmen and workers find their stocks of merchandise increased beyond desired levels, both directly through the suppliers' reduced sales and indirectly through the suppliers' own reduced demand for stocks, investment, and consumption goods. The reaction of business throughout the economy to these developments is the laying off of workers, which in turn causes the disappearance of additional purchasing power, resulting in a vicious circle, until renewed bumper crops and increased sales start the economy on a beneficia cycle.

Temporary or permanent reductions in aggregate demand affect the international trade balance in this fashion because of a phenomenon that is known as the marginal propensity to import. It has been observed that at constant relative price levels between countries, a given country's imports tend to vary roughly proportionately with its income. Thus, a country whose imports fall by $15 million when its income level is lowered by $100 million is known to have a marginal propensity to import equal to 0·15, which is normally constant over a wide range of income changes.

An application of these ideas to the problem of adjustments under the gold standard leads to the following simplified pattern of events. The assumed failure of the harvest immediately and directly reduces national income.

Along with this income reduction occurs a fall in imports, representing initially only those foreign products the farmers otherwise would have purchased. Soon, however, other business activities are curtailed, national income falls and imports are reduced further. If the unemployment following the initial disturbance and the import propensity are great enough, the resultant lowering of imports can eliminate all deficits that would have appeared otherwise and thus reduce the need for actual international movements of gold.[2]

During the periods when the gold standard was actually working in the world, price flexibility decreased progressively and the Keynesian income fluctuations increased, both along with the rise in general industrialization and unionization. Empirically, therefore, income adjustments tended to be more important during the last decade of the nineteenth and early twentieth century than they were before.

A third explanation of the Taussig findings complements the other and does not change the basic classical model in a significant manner. It is recalled that the preceding analysis assumed that gold was the only money in the economy, and that there was a one-to-one correspondence between gold lost in balance-of-payments deficits and reductions in domestic money supplies. This system is also known as the 'gold specie' standard.

In the real world, these conditions never prevailed strictly. Even when gold coins made up the bulk of the

2. Logically, the deficit country's reduced imports cause a decrease in aggregate demand in the rest of the world, which through the action of the multiplier lowers equilibrium income there. However, this lower income in the rest of the world causes a decrease of imports from the original deficit country via the mechanism of the marginal propensity to import. As a result of this decrease in exports the aggregate demand in the deficit country is reduced further still and leads to additional income–import repercussions in the rest of the world. These repercussions have been shown to represent an infinite series, of which the individual steps tend to become rapidly very small and can be neglected under a wide range of plausible assumptions. See Machlup (1943). The basic analysis of the gold standard mechanism under the assumption of Keynesian income changes is not affected in any significant way by neglect of these international income repercussions.

hand-to-hand money, fractional coins often consisted of some other metal or substitute and major transactions were frequently carried out through the shipment of drafts and cheques substituting for the actual gold. The existence and the proliferation of these gold substitutes serving as money eventually loosened the one-to-one link between changes in a nation's gold stock and money supply. However, the essential feature of the system was retained in the sense that all forms of monetary assets could readily be exchanged into gold. The resultant system is known as the 'gold bullion' standard.

Quantitatively the most important source of gold substitutes was the banking system and the demand deposits it created. However, because gold tended to serve as the liquidity reserve of the banking system, any changes in a country's stock of monetary gold influenced these reserves and the quantity of demand deposits outstanding. In fact, because of the multiple expansion of deposits on the gold base, a given change in the gold stock normally had a multiple effect on the total money supply, and, for this analytically highly important reason, relatively small flows of monetary gold between countries were capable of producing the kind of reductions in the money supply and price levels under the gold bullion standard which the basic classical model of the gold specie standard envisaged.

The theoretical models explaining international payments and adjustments under the gold standard just presented are analytical prototypes. In the real world there existed a blend of all four: internal disturbances would tend to cause domestic price changes and flows of gold between countries. But there would also be amplified effects on national supplies of credit money. Short-term capital flows would reduce the need for price changes and gold flows. Income effects would tend to influence balance of payments through changes in the demand for imports. However, logically and for the sake of easy exposition it is useful to distinguish these four elements of the adjustment process. One of the main features of this adjustment process, it is worth pointing out, is its automaticity and the absence of any governmental activity.

In recent empirical studies of the gold standard two additional important elements of this theoretical construct have been considered. The first of these elements concerns the role of government discretionary policies in the operation of the system. The government policies relevant in this context are those of exchange rate revaluation, in the form of redefining the gold value of domestic currency, and monetary policy, in the form of changing the quantity of money or the cost of credit. A. Bloomfield (1959), in an important study of actual government policies during the period 1880–1914, which he considers to be the time when the gold standard was most firmly established in the world, discovered that governments did in fact occasionally vary the price at which they purchased or sold gold bullion in rather subtle and discrete ways. For example, countries would sometimes open offices for the purchase of bullion in border cities, lowering the cost of gold shipment and thus encouraging the importation of gold from neighbouring countries at the outwardly fixed and unchanged unit price. In general, however, such interferences were rare and quantitatively insignificant.

In the realm of monetary policy, governments had more range for important actions because gold flows through their effect on bank reserves had a direct connexion with countries' supplies of credit money. To prevent severe credit contractions, financial crises and unemployment, central banks, through discretionary open market operations, could offset gold losses and by maintaining the base on which the credit money was built, prevent the contraction and other disruptions of the economy from taking place. Bloomfield's study revealed that in fact central banks seemed to engage in such offsetting policies quite frequently. However, it is clear that as long as these policies did not neutralize completely the effects of the gold losses, and instead only lessened their influence, the basic working of the system is not destroyed but only slowed down. Changes in discount rates were similarly used by governments to reduce the domestic impact of gold flows by reinforcing the interest rate mechanism and directing private capital flows in the manner suggested in the basic model. Natural catastrophes and gold losses, for example, under the model discussed above would lead to interest rate increases and private capital inflows which governments could speed up or reinforce through the appropriate increase in its discount rate. Ultimately, the most important question about the role of these government policies is whether in fact they prevented basic adjustments and caused periods of disequilibrium with all their manifestations such as unemployment, revaluations, the imposition of tariffs and other restrictions on trade. The evidence suggests clearly that government policies did not cause these effects and that while they may have modified the working of the gold standard system, they did not alter it basically from the way the theoretical blueprints suggest.

The second important element of the real world concerned the central role of Britain which at the time dominated world trade and finance as no other country has since. Because of this position of dominance, Britain enjoyed an exceedingly high interest elasticity of private capital flows, so that a slight change in the discount rate was sufficient to alter the balance of payments by significant amounts. In the framework of the basic models introduced above, such management of private capital flows merely serves to minimize the flow of gold and while it slowed down the fundamental adjustment process, it did not prevent it from working altogether. If a deficit in the balance of payments is reduced by an increase in the discount rate, the increased level of interest rates at the same time restricts domestic demand, lowers prices and thus restores equilibrium in foreign trade, and vice versa for reductions in the discount rate. For small rises in the discount rate the resultant adjustments were small also and a given required basic adjustment took longer to be completed.

R. Triffin (1947) suggested in a study that the adjustment process in the case of British deficits may not have worked by restricting domestic demand, but by improving Britain's terms of trade in the following way. The cost of credit was an important factor in determining the size of physical stocks of raw materials held in Britain. As the discount rate was raised, new purchases of raw materials fell off and the resultant glut of products abroad caused a lowering of their prices, improving Britain's terms of trade and balance-of-payments. The burden of adjustment in real terms to a British disequilibrium thus fell primarily on the rest of the world rather than on Britain, and the rest of the world in more equal measure as the basic model suggests. Triffin may be correct in his analysis of the nineteenth century gold standard experience, though more work needs to be done on the historic development of prices and interest rates to clinch the case. However, this finding does not invalidate the theoretical analysis of the gold standard mechanism in a world of roughly equal sized countries, which was presented above and which is relevant for the current discussion of the alternative forms of monetary organization.

History of the Gold Standard

Implicit in the analytical models of the gold standard just presented is the dual role of gold as, first, a means of settling payments imbalances between nations and, second, the standard of value to which all national currencies are linked. The institutional arrangements under which gold can play these roles exist when national governments purchase and sell gold bullion and mint gold coin in unlimited quantities at fixed prices, and when there are no legal obstacles on the melting of coin or export of the bullion.

Historically gold coins have circulated since antiquity,

but these formal institutional requirements of the gold standard were not met until the development of strong national governments in Western Europe during the eighteenth and nineteenth centuries. One of the most serious obstacles in the development of the gold standard was the fact that gold and silver coins had circulated side by side for many centuries so that when governments began to assert their monetary sovereignty they were forced to establish ratios of exchange for gold and silver bullion. Depending on the ratio chosen and technological developments in the production and industrial use of the two metals at various times, one or the other tended to be overvalued and drove the other metal from circulation, as a result of the working of Gresham's famous law.

Great Britain was the first major country to meet the formal conditions of being on the gold standard when in 1821 the Bank of England was legally required to redeem its notes in gold bars or coin, and when all prohibition on melting of coin and export of gold were repealed. Around 1850 the world price of gold fell relative to silver when supplies from the newly discovered fields in California and Australia came on the market. As a further result, in the United States and France Gresham's law caused the disappearance of silver coins and the two countries moved from the bimetallic standard to the *de facto* gold standard. Belgium, Switzerland and Italy had standard monetary units equal to those of France and also went on to the gold standard at the same time. However, by 1870 some countries such as Germany were still on the silver standard and wars and revolutions had forced other countries into issuing inconvertible currencies. Among the latter group of countries were Russia, Austria-Hungary, Italy and the United States. After the Franco–Prussian war of 1870, however, Germany obtained sufficient gold payments from France as reparations to enable her to adopt a genuine gold standard, and during the following decade a sufficiently large number of the remaining major countries of the world had passed the necessary legislation, so that many observers consider the year 1880 as the beginning of the 'universal' gold standard era. Strictly speaking, however, Russia, Austria-Hungary, India and Japan met the gold standard requirements only after 1895 and for this reason some observers put the beginning of the gold standard era as late as 1900.

The exact beginning of the gold standard era is not really very important because its effective life, ending with the outbreak of the First World War hostilities in 1914, was perhaps fifteen or thirty-five years and thus represents even at maximum a very short span in the history of the world or even of the industrialized West. Yet, the period is remembered with nostalgia by many people and some influential economists and politicians have urged that it be reinstituted in the 1960s. Why, then, is this period of the gold standard held in such high esteem?

The answer to this question is to be found in the standard's alleged record of performance in contributing to an increase in the welfare of mankind. Human welfare has many dimensions but two of the most important are the level and stability of real income and the degree to which individuals are free to shape their own destiny. With respect to the first, the last half of the nineteenth century saw a remarkable growth in *per capita* real income, which was made possible through the techniques of mass production, the falling of food prices caused by the opening of the North American prairies and the availability of low cost steamship and railroad transportation. Economic stability was reasonably great, interrupted only by occasional depressions and financial crises. Even during the long period of falling world prices in the 1880s and 1890s *per capita* incomes continued to rise. In the decade following the California gold discoveries in 1849 and after the Alaska discoveries and the development of the cyanide process for refining South African gold about 1895 gold production increased rapidly and caused world prices to rise. These inflations created a sense of well-being in business and the general public throughout the world. The gold standard *contributed* to these developments by encouraging an efficient allocation of resources and pattern of development. During the gold standard era goods were exchanged freely in international trade so that production tended to locate in technically optimum places; capital flowed to wherever productivity was highest without restrictions and in the confidence that world prices would be stable.

In the second important area of human welfare, the last half of the nineteenth century saw the movement towards greater personal and political freedom. Governments by and large pursued policies of enlightened nationalism, channeling peoples' energies into economic development and industrialization, permitting individuals a maximum of freedom to move geographically, to choose occupations and to advance themselves socially. As compared with the level of government activities in the economy prevailing during the preceding period of mercantilism and the following period of neo-mercantilism and nationalism of the 1930s, government activity during the gold standard was at a minimum. Most important, governments acted as if they were part of a world community, obeying rules of behaviour that served the purposes of a smoothly functioning international economy. In cases of conflict between the interests of the world community and domestic welfare, the latter was subordinated to the former. Such internationalist policies did not have the same serious consequences for domestic welfare at that time as they would at present, because the degree of industrialization was lower and consequently any slow-down in business activity would typically affect the living standards of smaller proportions of the population. For all of these reasons the gold standard period is considered by many as having been a desirable one in which to live, and one worth recreating for the present world.

This favourable interpretation of the gold standard's history has been challenged, and it is not clear to what extent the international monetary organization of the time was responsible for the growth in world welfare, and to what extent the preceding description of the 'good old times' of the late nineteenth century made the mistake of confusing causes and effects. It can easily be argued that the real causes of the observed increases in over-all well-being were the movement of Western societies towards democracy and the acceleration of industrial development taking place for other reasons. The gold standard, from this point of view, merely was a passive agent, facilitating but not influencing in any meaningful way this development. Subsequent growth in many of the world's economies, especially the rapid gains in real income in the United States, Western Europe and the Soviet Union since the end of the Second World War, suggest strongly that the gold standard is not a necessary condition for real economic development.

But what about personal liberty, freedom from government intervention which characterized economic growth under the gold standard and which was restricted to varying degrees in the rapid growth situations after the Second World War? Would a gold standard in this period have enabled the world to make the same gains in income without this loss of personal liberty and this growth of government activism in the economy? It is doubtful that it would have done so. Government involvement in capitalistic economies had become necessary because of the nature and complexity of the twentieth-century industrial structure, which requires the provision of public goods in quantities not technically feasible or necessary in the nineteenth century. The taxation and expenditures caused by these public goods makes government activism unavoidable. Moreover, the modern industrial economies are subject to at least the same instabilities as were the economies of the nineteenth century, but because of the populations' greater size and dependence on industrial employment, they create much greater human misery than did the same fluctuations in the nineteenth century. As the analysis of this chapter has shown, the working of the gold standard involves surrender by national governments of the right to engage in domestic stabilizing policies that are in conflict with the economic forces set in motion by the payments deficits and gold flows. Governments are not, and because of the severity of welfare losses should not, be willing to give up the rights to engage in these policies. Standards of government activity, optimum personal and economic liberty set under the technical conditions prevailing in the nineteenth century are not applicable in the twentieth century. And neither is the gold standard with which they are associated.

6 Freely Fluctuating Exchange Rates

The Basic Model

The case for freely fluctuating exchange rates is as simple and as powerful as the case for the free market economy in general. They both promote an efficient allocation of resources at least cost. Adam Smith demonstrated how individuals seeking to serve their own self-interest are led by 'the invisible hand' of the market place to serve the interest of all, tending to lead the economy to the condition where no one person can be made better off, without making someone else worse off. In so doing the market solves a vastly complicated problem of determining relative prices, of choosing optimum technology, of recognizing, measuring and satisfying the needs of all economic units while compensating them for the appropriate social value of their contribution to the satisfaction of these needs, all without planning and the requirement for any government agency to collect, interpret and act upon the basic knowledge necessary for the solution of this problem. Since Adam Smith's intellectually and ideologically powerful analysis of how the invisible hand works, the basic argument has been examined carefully and a large body of knowledge has been amassed, specifying the conditions under which the analysis is valid. Students of economics are well aware that the invisible hand fulfils its functions completely only if there is perfect competition in all markets, and that the economy's efficiency is reduced by the existence of monopolies, monopolistic competition, public goods, externalities and price rigidities and that the free market's income distribution may be socially undesirable. The importance of these modifications of the free market model are constantly re-evaluated, both theoretically and empirically, and frequently governments attempt to rectify major shortcomings in the market system through appropriate policies. In general, however, the capitalist countries of the West retain a basic practical reliance on the market's ability to solve the problems of pricing and of the allocation of scarce resources.

The intellectual case for freely fluctuating exchange rates arises directly from the general argument for the efficiency of a free market system. From this point of view exchange rates are nothing but prices which, if determined freely in the market with all other prices, assure the efficient allocation of resources throughout the world. Governments are not required to make judgements about correct exchange rates, thus saving the cost of information gathering, and policy implementation. They never make any 'wrong' decisions and never face balance-of-payments crises. Consequently, they never have to meet payments imbalances through restrictions on trade, changes of domestic prices and income, interest rates and capital flows, in the manner analysed in chapter 2 above.

Just as Adam Smith's idea of the indivisible hand has been analysed in great detail and its validity has been found to depend upon the fulfilment of various conditions, so has the argument for freely flexible exchange rates been criticized at length. The remainder of this chapter is devoted to a discussion of the arguments for and against the universal adoption of freely flexible rates, using the following approach. At first, each argument against the use of flexible exchange rates is stated as strongly as possible. This statement is then critically examined as to its theoretical validity and empirical content. This method of presentation was chosen since it resembles the real world conditions encountered by the advocates of a régime of freely fluctuating rates, who find themselves in the position of having to answer the theoretical and practical objections of those who are defending the present system of pegged but adjustable rates. The reason why the advocates of flexible rates are in this position is found in the historic development of the current system. The discussion of the gold standard in the last chapter showed how the world moved from the freely circulating gold coins requiring no government involvement at all, to the system whose success depended on government's willingness to exchange paper currency into bullion at a fixed and never changing price. Logically and practically it is only a small step from the latter arrangements to the present ones, where the gold value of a currency is adjusted whenever its existing price in terms of gold results in persistent excess demand or supply conditions. Mainly as a result of this historic development, the present system is so deeply entrenched that its advocates are in a position to put the burden of proof about the workability of freely flexible exchange rates upon those favouring the change.

Before moving to the discussion of the arguments about the workability of flexible exchange rates, one important point needs to be clarified. When in this chapter reference is made to 'freely fluctuating rates', it is to a régime where governments refrain *completely* from any activities in the exchange markets. Not all protagonists of flexible exchange rates envision the same arrangements. There are some who wish governments to stabilize exchange rates in the short run, evening out day-to-day fluctuations, but never blocking the realization of any fundamental trends in the price of foreign exchange. This system is a hybrid of pegged rates and freely fluctuating rates and has many of the undesirable properties of both systems and nearly all of the objections to perfectly flexible rates discussed below apply to it. It has the disadvantage of requiring governments to form judgements about the appropriate level of the exchange rate at any given moment of time, since it is necessary to know whether an observed price trend is merely temporary or fundamental. This task is made more difficult by the actions of speculators who, just as under the system of pegged rates, try to judge not only market trends but also any pending government actions. For these reasons the following discussion contemplates the merits of a system of exchange rates free to fluctuate without any government intervention in the exchange market.

The Problem of Real Costs and Uncertainty

1. Costs of transition period

Contention: The switchover from pegged rates to flexible rates is bound to be accompanied by chaos in the exchange markets, upsetting international patterns of trade and capital flows, causing in turn upheavals in many domestic markets. Empirical evidence suggesting the likelihood of these events is very strong. Their real social cost tends to be very large, and it might take a long time of superior performance by the flexible exchange rate system to amortize this cost of transition.

Answer: The chaos resulting from the transition is a once-and-for-all cost while the benefits can be expected to last for as long as the system is maintained, so that even if initial costs are high there may be a substantial positive return to the introduction of flexible rates. Furthermore, the cost should be compared with the sum of the costs incurred by the chaos accompanying the revaluation of major currencies under the pegged system. It is not legitimate to set up a smoothly functioning system of pegged rates as a standard of comparison but instead the proper base of comparison should be the historic performance record of the system the flexible rates are to replace. Moreover, the chaos expected to follow from a sudden freeing of all exchange rates could be reduced considerably by the use of policies specifically designed to cope with transitional problems. For example, countries could introduce universal flexibility by the gradual widening of intervention margins and by progressive limitations on the frequency and intensity of pegging operations.

The available historical evidence suggests that frequently the introduction of flexible exchange rates has been accompanied by chaos, in internal and external economic conditions. However, it is highly misleading to infer from this simultaneity of events the causal relationship running from the introduction of the rates to the chaotic conditions. Historically, domestic inflation and the mismanagement of external accounts, often caused by wars and their aftermath, has tended to lead to such difficulties for governments that flexible exchange rates were the only solution. Without their use the chaos might have been greater still. See also the discussion of destabilizing speculation, below, for more details about the historic circumstances surrounding the episodes when freely fluctuating exchange rates were in actual use.

2. Cost of trade

Contention: For most people price uncertainty represents a disutility and therefore the increased frequency and magnitude of exchange rate fluctuations, under the absence of government stabilization policies, causes them to be made worse off. While it is true that the most important uncertainty for traders, the price changes between commitment to accept delivery of, or make payment in, foreign currency and the actual transaction, can be eliminated through the sale or purchase of forward contracts, this activity involves a real cost in the form of resource transfers to those willing to bear the exchange risk. This cost of eliminating uncertainty enters the price of internationally traded goods and tends to reduce the level of trade and specialization in the same way as do costs of transportation and insurance. Such limitations on the opportunity to gain from trade lowers world welfare below the level attainable without the price uncertainty.

Answer: Again it is necessary to establish an appropriate basis for comparing the level of uncertainty under flexible exchange rates. Under pegged rates, the public is also confronted with considerable uncertainty stemming from fluctuations of the price within the limits set by the official intervention points, from occasional adjustments in the peg, from trade and exchange restrictions, and greater volatility in domestic conditions arising when monetary or fiscal policies are used to balance external accounts. Only empirical experience can provide information necessary to make meaningful judgements about the relative levels of traders' uncertainty under the two systems.

The argument about the transfer of real resources to agents absorbing the exchange risk, is based on a theoretical misconception and is not supported by empirical evidence. Theoretically, existing uncertainty about future exchange rates prompts both exporters and importers to enter the forward exchange market. Foreign exchange dealers' task is the matching of the demand and supply of *forward* exchange by the exporters and importers, in the same way they match the demand and supply of spot exchange under pegged rates. These agents do not have to bear the exchange risk, except for small day-to-day margins when market demand and supply do not match exactly. Empirically, there exists no evidence that foreign exchange dealers increased their share of national income when flexible exchange rates were in effect in Canada during the period 1950–62.

Lastly, the ultimate test of the proposition that flexibility of exchange rates reduces the level of trade lies in the actual observation of events during periods when some countries actually refrained from pegging their currency. The empirical evidence is not easy to interpret because of the existence of many other simultaneous developments bearing on the level of trade during, before and after the period of exchange rate flexibility. However, after careful analysis of the available data, several economists have concluded that there is no evidence that flexible rates themselves have had negative effects on the level of international trade.

3. Reduction in capital flows

Contention: Flexible exchange rates reduce international long term capital movements because they result in greater uncertainty about the value and yield of foreign investments. Capital losses caused by domestic inflation and the accompanying depreciation of the borrowing country's currency can easily wipe out any interest advantage foreign investments initially offered to the lender. This private uncertainty of assets denominated in foreign currency reduces the flow of capital and thus lowers the total social productivity of the world's stock of physical capital.

Answer: Only foreign investments denominated in foreign currency and bearing fixed interest are subject to capital losses due to inflation in the borrowing country and the accompanying devaluation of the currency. Direct foreign investment and equity portfolio assets appreciate along with domestic inflation and currency depreciation and therefore tend to maintain the investor's original real purchasing power. Because exchange rate changes have these different effects on bonds and equity capital, the institution of freely fluctuating rates probably would lead to more foreign equity financing at the expense of bond flotations. Furthermore, the market probably would develop bonds which maintain the real value of the lender's capital through the introduction of either adjustment clauses for capital value changes resulting from inflation, or the denomination of the capital sum and interest payments in the lender's or some other stable country's currency.

It cannot be established theoretically whether these kinds of changes in international lending expected to take place under a régime of freely fluctuating exchange rates, would be sufficient to maintain capital flows at the level found during the gold standard or under a system of pegged but adjustable rates. However, it is quite clear that under pegged rates foreign investments are subject to many of the same dangers as under flexible rates, especially in the sense that foreign countries have domestic inflations and devalue their currencies. In addition, empirical evidence suggests that under pegged rates frequently countries interfere with the free movement of private long term capital for purposes of achieving balance-of-payments equilibrium. These barriers to the free flow of capital may well be at least as harmful for the world wide efficient distribution of capital, as would be any reduction following the adoption of freely fluctuating exchange rates.

Problems Concerning Elasticities

1. Elasticity pessimism

Contention: The price elasticities of import demand for internationally traded goods are low. If they are so low that the Marshall–Lerner condition is not fulfilled, and the elasticity of demand for a country's imports and the elasticity of the world's demand for its exports sum to less than one, then a country's trade balance fails to improve if its exchange rate depreciates, and depreciation alone does not restore balance. Even if the sum of import elasticities is greater than one, generally low elasticities imply that the attainment of any proportionate balance-of-trade improvements require large proportionate changes in exchange rates. Such wide fluctuations are an impediment to international trace and capital flows for reasons discussed above under the titles Cost of Trade and Reduction in capital flows.

Answer: There is very little empirical evidence to suggest that the import elasticities facing one country are very low. At times in the past when countries did not experience improvements in their balance of payments after devaluation, they normally had failed to engage in the necessary policies for domestic expenditure reduction or switching. As a result, aggregate demand continued to exceed aggregate supply and the basic cause of the deficit was not removed and wiped out the otherwise beneficial effects of the devaluation.

The belief in the existence of high elasticities is based on both theoretical and empirical evidence. While it is true that the elasticity of world demand for any one product may not be high, the demand elasticity for any one country's output of that product is high. Thus, for example, the world consumption of tea probably would increase by less than 10 per cent if tea prices would fall by 10 per cent. However, if *one* country would lower the price at which it is willing to sell tea by 10 per cent below the prevailing world price for the identical quality product, it could sell all it can produce domestically. As to empirical evidence, econometric measurement of demand elasticities in recent years have found elasticities to be quite high.

In general it is true that demand elasticities are a function of time. A day after reduction in the price of tea by one supplier, his sales can be expected to increase only little because the price change may not be known or because buyers have stocks of tea or are contractually bound to deliveries from other higher priced sources. But after some time the price reduction will be known widely in the market, consumers' stocks need to be replenished, existing contracts between buyers and sellers come up for renewal, and buyers will take advantage of the lower price in increasing quantity. Because of this fact a given disequilibrium in foreign demand would tend to cause initially wide price movements, which eventually tend to be narrowed as the forces responsible for high trade elasticities in the long run come into effect. How big might these initial fluctuations be?

First, it must be remembered that very rarely are there events which suddenly affect a country's balance of trade. Bad harvests, technical change, domestic inflations, show their disequilibrating effects slowly. As a result, the factors causing trade elasticities to be high have sufficient time to operate. Second, even if payments disturbances are not gradual, the resultant persistent patterns of prices as are suggested by the analysis of elasticities through time tend to be exploited by speculators. Knowing that the exchange rate will fall after its initial rise, they sell it at the high and repurchase it at the low price. In so doing, of course, speculators prevent the rise in price from becoming as high as it would have been otherwise and thus stabilize the exchange rate.

2. Destabilizing speculation

Contention: Foreign exchange speculation makes a system of freely fluctuating exchange rates unstable. Once an exchange rate begins to depreciate speculators will have the tendency to expect further depreciation. Acting upon these expectations asset holders sell the currency, exporters slow down sales and payments and importers speed up purchases and payments. This speculative activity causes further currency depreciation, causes speculators' expectations to be realized and feeds further speculation in a cumulative, vicious cycle in which speculators make their own expectations come true. Even if the process is not infinitely cumulative, speculators are bound to cause large swings in exchange rates which are an impediment to international trade and capital flows, for the reasons discussed above.

Answer: The arguments about the cumulative process of self-fulfilling speculation are not well founded. Consider a situation where asset holders, exporters and importers have engaged in their activities for one week and they have in fact forced a decrease in the exchange rate. In the following week asset holders have fewer assets to draw upon, interest rates at which speculative funds can be borrowed have risen, exporters and importers face lowered domestic and higher foreign prices and also meet higher domestic interest rates at which to finance their payments leads and lags. All of these 'real forces' ultimately set a limit to the asset holders' and traders' ability to carry on their speculative activities. Only if a government, through inflationary policies, keeps interest rates low and domestic goods prices high and thus prevents these real forces from developing can there be a cumulative depreciation of the currency. Under these circumstances the blame for the domestic inflation and exchange rate depreciation should be put on the government's inflationary policies, not on the speculators.

If real forces work without impediment, and speculators through faulty judgements sell at lower prices than those warranted by existing world-wide conditions of prices, demand and supply, then the speculators lose money on their activities. In the long run speculators who have a tendency to misjudge real forces drop out of the market, and only those speculators who are capable of forecasting 'normal' prices remain active. This group of speculators serves a socially useful function of evening out temporary fluctuations. For example, if a country's harvest fails and the exchange rate falls, speculators anticipating the future exchange rate to return to its 'normal' level after the next harvest buy currency at the price below normal in expectation of profits from future sales. As a result the price falls less than it would have in the absence of the speculators' purchases, who, from a social point of view, are 'lending' resources to the country to overcome the temporary effects of a bad harvest.

It has been argued that the elimination of destabilizing unsuccessful speculators, predicted by the theory, does not take place effectively since dropouts always tend to be replaced by new entrants willing to risk their capital, so that at all times there exists a 'floating' population of destabilizing speculators. Such a phenomenon is theoretically possible.[1] However, the entire controversy over the effects of speculation on foreign currencies can ultimately be settled only through experience. Unfortunately, the evidence drawn from past experience is mixed. The Canadian

---

1. It has also been shown that some speculators can profit consistently even though their purchases and sales add to price instability. See Baumol (1957 and 1959). To derive these results very strong assumptions about the speculators' behavior and price forecasting abilities have to be made, though the logical possibility represents an important qualification of the basic arguments about profitability of speculation and stability.

exchange rate did not suffer greatly from speculative instabilities, but it is not clear to what extent this has been due to limited government intervention. Other historic experiments with the use of freely flexible exchange rates have nearly always been accompanied by unsettling speculation. However, these experiments are not really a fair test since they were always introduced after major economic crises and after conventional pegging operations proved totally inadequate to deal with the problems. The best known experiments in this category are those when the United States did not maintain stable exchange rates with gold standard countries from the Civil War until 1879, and when several European countries let their currencies float after the First World War, until restoration of a quasi gold standard in the twenties.

In general, the uncertainty of the effects speculators are likely to have on freely floating exchange rates is, undoubtedly, one of the most important obstacles standing in the way of the widespread adoption of floating rates. In other markets, such as for corporate securities, commodities, speculators frequently do engage in unsettling activities. However, it should be noted that such speculation for the most part takes place in relatively thin markets where speculators' limited resources have the greatest leverage. This fact has an important implication for flexible exchange rates also in that it suggests stability might be greater the deeper a market, and the larger the geographic area within which rates are fixed and whose external rate is free to fluctuate. These considerations will be taken up below under the title 'optimum currency areas'.

Problems Involving Political Judgements

1. The anchor argument

Contention: In democracies elected officials face the temptation to use economic policies to assure re-election. Low levels of unemployment and the temporary euphoria accompanying periods of inflation are particularly useful methods of achieving these ends. Yet inflation in the long run is bad for the economy and the moral and ethical values of society. For this reason many Western governments have independent monetary authorities and other institutional arrangements, serving to isolate economic policy making from short-run political manipulation. Fixed exchange rates have traditionally helped national monetary authorities in their fight for price stability, because inflation tends to cause payments deficits and reserve losses, which the guardians of price stability then used as a justification for the imposition of monetary and fiscal stringency and the slow down in the rate of inflation. Under flexible exchange rates international payments deficits would never occur, and monetary authorities would lose their anchor restraining monetary expansion.

Answer: This argument about the disadvantages of flexible exchange rates is based on a rather cynical view of democratic processes, namely the idea that central bankers or other economic technicians know better what rate of inflation is in the long-run interest of a nation than does the public. Price stability is not a constitutional right. Politicians and the government executive should be sensitive to the public's desired relative quantities of inflation and unemployment. If the public wants to trade some unemployment for a somewhat higher rate of inflation, and makes this preference known by electing candidates who stand for such a policy, it ought to be able to do so without being encumbered by monetary, or any other anchors, thrown out by conservative elements in society. From this point of view the loss of the monetary anchor, implied by the institution of flexible exchange rates, is a blessing rather than a disadvantage.

2. Internationalist argument

Contention: It is no coincidence that internationalism was strongest during the period of the gold standard in the nineteenth century. The level of international financial integration was high, and successful operation of the system of fixed exchange rates requires substantial inter-governmental consultation and co-operation. This internationalism helped to raise world welfare by permitting people and capital to move between countries with relative ease. Flexible exchange rates, on the other hand, would encourage nationalism by making it easier for governments to pursue policies without regard for the consequences to other countries. In such a world governments would tend to compete with each other in many ways, in the process erecting barriers to the free circulation of people and capital.

Answer: As it was argued in the discussion of the gold standard, countries began to renounce this system because industrialization and downward rigidity of wages made internationalism socially too costly. The gold standard worked because other necessary conditions for internationalism were right and not because there was a gold standard. It is, therefore, an illusion to believe that rigid exchange rates or the gold standard would bring an end to the current wave of nationalism. In the same way, flexible exchange rates would probably do little to increase nationalism.

However, fixed exchange rates have caused the erection of many controls on trade and capital movements which appear to be manifestations of nationalism, but in reality have been motivated by balance-of-payments problems. Many of these barriers to trade and capital flows may be eliminated once flexible exchange rates bring to an end all balance-of-payments problems. It may well be that such economic liberalization would be an important aid to greater international economic integration and co-operation than exists under the system of the adjustable peg.

The Problem of Optimum Currency Areas

The traditional debate over the merits and faults of a system of freely floating exchange rates, summarized in the preceding part of this chapter, has recently been enriched by an important contribution by Robert A. Mundell (1961). He raised the question about the optimum geographic area within which exchange rates are fixed, but whose external price of currency is free to float. Certainly there is nothing sacrosanct about the historically determined national borders and currencies.

For example, if flexible exchange rates were to be introduced on a world-wide scale, should the principality of Luxemburg have its own currency? Luxemburg could then readily engage in domestic monetary and fiscal policies to attain whatever social objectives it sets for itself, without any fear of balance of payments problems. But if flexible rates are so beneficial to Luxemburg, why not provide the U.S. state of West Virginia with its own floating currency, and permit its government to solve its problems of chronic unemployment?

The concept of optimum currency areas is easier to describe than to analyse and embody in policy prescriptions. Geographers have long known the concept of optimum geographic areas, but economists appear to have been confused in their use of the concept by the fact that optimality has many dimensions. A given geographic area may be optimal in the sense that it achieves the inclusion of all peoples of the same ethnic and cultural background, or it may be optimal with respect to the distribution of resources and climate such as to give an economy greatest economic stability, or it may be optimal in the sense of permitting least cost of production and distribution as a result of providing the opportunity to exploit economies of scale without crowding, etc.

Mundell's main analysis focused on optimality in the sense of an area's ability to make easy domestic adjustments to exogeneous disequilibria in the balance of payments. He thus argued that areas within which factors of production can move readily or are distributed uniformly should make up one currency unit because balance-of-payments deficits can be corrected easily by shifting resources between industries, according to conditions of international demand. For example, coal mining regions typically do not have resource endowments similar to those in their neighbouring territories, and coal miners have little geographic and occupational mobility. Therefore, a down-turn in the demand for coal tends to be difficult to absorb through intra-regional adjustments. A separate currency and flexible exchange rate for the coal mining area facilitates maintenance of full employment through lowering of the export price of coal, and from this point of view a coal mining region represents an optimum currency area.

Ronald McKinnon (1963) expanded on another criterion of optimality mentioned briefly by Mundell, namely that the region's monetary assets should have sufficiently stable values to serve as an acceptable medium of exchange and asset to the wealth-holders in the region. Thus, if the coal region mentioned in the preceding example is small, the coal miners' efforts to maintain their standard of living in real terms, which tends to be reduced by the increased cost of imports caused by the currency depreciation, lead to higher nominal wages and a constantly depreciating exchange rate. As a result, the domestic currency of the region is subjected to a loss of purchasing power and becomes an unattractive asset to hold. Demand for monetary assets denominated in foreign currency by wealth-holders in that region causes the exchange rate to depreciate further and generally may add to the system's instability. In the discussion above, a new concept of optimality has been suggested. It argues that a currency area should be large enough so that the total quantity of foreign exchange transactions per time period will also be large relative to resources of speculators who will consequently find it difficult to influence currency prices in a consistently de-stabilizing manner.

All of these criteria are vague. What degree of factor mobility, what stability of currency values are to be attained in the optimum currency area? Similarly, if all potential speculators in the world would use their resources to attack one currency, there is really no imaginable size of currency area that can resist such price pressures. Moreover, what relative weights should be given to these criteria of optimality if optimum currency areas determined under each should be different, as they are likely to be? What weight should be given to social, political, historical criteria for optimality?

At the present there appear to be no satisfactory, scientifically valid answers to the problems raised in connexion with the concept of optimum currency areas. Yet, intuitively, most observers agree that the long-run success of a universal system of flexible exchange rates may not be independent of the choice of areas whose currency values are free to fluctuate in relation with each other. One might envisage, for example, that the world be divided into four major currency areas. First, the Americas, where all of the smaller nations of North and South America maintain a rigid peg with respect to the U.S. dollar. Second, a European area where the Common Market and European Free Trade Area countries maintain rigid pegs among their currencies. Affiliated with this block might be countries of Africa and perhaps of the Middle East. Third, an East Pacific area anchored by Japan and Australia, including perhaps South East Asia, New Zealand and the Philippines. A fourth block might consist of the Indian subcontinent. Such institutional arrangements would encourage maximum economic integration among trading partners related to each other through geographic proximity, ethnic and cultural ties as well as historic economic interdependence. At the same time, the freely fluctuating rates between the blocks would give each freedom from balance-of-payments considerations not enjoyed at present, thus permitting each area to pursue optimum monetary and fiscal policies. Within the areas can be found sufficiently large diversification of agricultural and industrial production, so that over-all demand for exports and imports probably would be rather stable. The absolute size of currency transactions would make it difficult for speculators to manipulate the exchange rates.

The Political Reality of Flexible Exchange Rates

In the view of many scholars who have studied the problem of freely fluctuating exchange rates, the analytical and empirical evidence suggests that world welfare would probably be increased significantly, if a system of freely fluctuating rates were substituted for the present system of pegged rates. There is no *certainty* that the welfare gains would be realized; economics, like other social sciences and unlike the physical sciences, cannot make laboratory experiments and 'prove' the validity of its propositions. However, the nature and size of the uncertainty is such that many economists think that the size of expected welfare gains is so great as to outweigh the expected value of possible losses.

Why then are flexible exchange rates not introduced? One reason lies in the unfortunate social lag between the discovery of knowledge in economics and the time taken by the public, and above all men in responsible positions, to carry out the change and integrate this knowledge into their systems of thoughts about the world. The role of deficit financing, as a method for stabilizing aggregate demand, required nearly 30 years between explicit formulation in economic models, and actual consistent use. Perhaps flexible exchange rates will have a better chance when the current generation of students are in positions of political and executive responsibility.

A second reason must be sought in the dual role of economists in society. On the one hand, their tasks are to use abstract reasoning to increase understanding of economic processes and to find 'ideal' solutions for the economic problems of society. In a sense, the preceding discussion of the flexible exchange rate controversy represents a summary of the past efforts along these lines. But on the other hand, economists are also needed as practical advisers to men of affairs, government officials who must decide what tomorrow's expenditures, taxes and price of gold should be. These government officials responsible to the party in power put great weight on not 'rocking the boat'. Their success is measured by the extent to which they are able to avoid crises, aiding re-election chances, and not by their innovative ability. Economists, who are advisers to these officials, in turn acquire a vested interest in seeing the marginal improvements of the system they recommended become successful. As a result of this dual role of economists in society, they present to the public a rather confusing picture of disagreement and disunity, and any opponent to reform can easily find some 'respected' economist and famous adviser to men of affairs, who is willing to speak out against the wisdom of introducing flexible exchange rates.

The Political Compromise of Flexibility Through a Rule

In recognition of the political difficulties facing all efforts aimed at introducing flexible exchange rates, economists have recently proposed a compromise set of institutional arrangements, which would give greater flexibility to exchange rates through time, but would have none of the alleged disadvantages of a régime of freely fluctuating rates. This proposal envisages maintenance of a system of parity exchange rates, like the one existing since the end of the Second World War under the Bretton Woods agreements. Countries would retain the responsibility of keeping their exchange rate within a margin of plus or minus one per cent around the agreed-upon par exchange value, through intervention in the foreign exchange markets.

However, under the proposed system the par value itself would be adjusted frequently and mechanically according to some agreed upon formula. Plans differ in detail, but the essential ingredient of the mechanism would be that daily exchange rates are averaged over a certain period in the past, say 360 days. The resultant moving average is then defined as being the official parity rate for the following day. If the average is computed by taking the geometric mean of daily observations over one year, then the maximum sustainable rate of change of an exchange rate is $\pm$ 2 per cent per year, given that rates are maintained within $\pm$ 1 per cent around par.[2] Maximum annual changes can be varied by changing the length of the averaging period and the size of the official intervention margins around par. Precise agreements on these matters would have to be reached by negotiations, which would probably result in a political compromise since technical economics is unable to suggest any rational criteria for choosing the maximum annual rates of change.

The main advantage of the system is that it permits gradual, but cumulatively significant, changes in the relative prices of currencies which correct fundamental payments disequilibria and reduce the need to hold international reserves, make domestic adjustments, impose direct controls, etc., in the manner discussed in Part One of this book.

Systematic and predictable exchange rate changes, which attract speculators under this system, could occur when a government permitted its exchange rate to be at the intervention point over the period of averaging. However, if the averaging period is long enough and the margins small enough, under these extreme conditions the day-to-day predictable maximum changes would tend to be very small and provide little opportunity for speculative

2. The formula for computing the maximum annual rate of change is $2\,b/a$, where b is the maximum between the registered par value and the market rate, and a is the number of years over which the averaging takes place. For a more detailed discussion of this formula see Black (1966).

profits to be made. Interest rates in the affected countries would tend to reflect the relative capital value losses resulting from holding assets denominated in that currency, so that normal capital flows would be unaffected by these predictable changes in the exchange rates. In practice, however, governments could be expected to keep market exchange rates pegged away from the intervention limits so that changes in official par would affect only the potential and not actual market rates. Speculators' efforts to out-guess government policies under these conditions would probably be no stronger or successful than they are under the present system of rigid par values.

Governments could use the system of a movable par value to change their exchange rates deliberately to increase employment, improve the terms of trade or accumulate unduly large quantities of reserves. These dangers of abuse are present in all systems of international monetary order except the theoretically pure gold standard and completely freely fluctuating rates. In any system of international economic relations where human judgement is involved, co-operation among nations is necessary and can keep such abuses to a minimum.

The proposal for the automatic adjustment of parity rates by an agreed-upon, predictable formula deserves careful attention by economists and politicians not as a step towards the introduction of freely fluctuating exchange rates, but as part of a programme for international monetary reform based upon systematizing the supply of international reserves. The next chapters discuss a number of prototypes for international monetary order based on the principle of systematic reserve increases.

7   The Gold Exchange Standard

The world monetary system which existed from the end of the Second World War until approximately 1968, is known as the gold exchange standard. The basic working characteristics of this form of world monetary order will be discussed first. Following are an analysis of its chief defects, a brief history of its actual operation, and a short analysis of proposals for its evolutionary reform.

The Theoretical Blueprint

The gold exchange standard evolved from the gold standard, but differs from it most basically in that under its operation international reserves consist of both gold and convertible national currencies. Consequently, the world's payment mechanism can function properly with a smaller quantity of gold than under the gold standard, thus economizing on the use of the precious metal. The gold exchange standard's most important features can best be demonstrated by the use of a simple model.

Consider a world consisting of many countries, one of which is called Banker and the rest are known as Other. All countries are assumed to have fixed exchange rates, independent monetary and fiscal systems, and thus have the need to hold international reserves for the settlement of payments imbalances, as was argued in Part One above. Initially, this world is assumed to be on a gold standard, using only gold to settle intercountry debts. Then the decision is made to institute the gold exchange standard, which requires the universal adoption of the following rules.

First, all gold held by Other countries is turned over to a Banker. Second, Banker issues to Other its own currency obligations, CO for short, in return for the gold and commits itself to hold only gold as reserves. The Banker obligations are convertible into gold on demand, and pay a low interest rate to bearer. Third, the national governments in Other agree to accept these Banker obligations as a means of payment, as they had previously accepted gold. Fourth, it is agreed that Banker can issue national obligations in excess of its gold stock as long as it maintains a minimum ratio of obligations to gold. Fifth, all newly mined gold not needed for industrial purposes is turned over to Banker at a predetermined, fixed price.

It is easy to see how such a system economizes on the use of gold. If Banker maintains a ratio of 25 per cent gold behind the obligations held by Other, then $100 of gold permits the existence of $400 of COs and a total stock of reserves of $500. The degree of economizing is greater, the smaller the ratio of gold to COs. In Figure 6 at time t_0 the initial stock of gold OG_0 is shown to support a

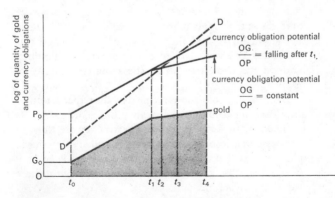

Figure 6. A model of the gold exchange standard

stock of currency obligations of G_0P_0, at an assumed ratio of OG/OP equal to 0.25.

The growth in the potential supply of COs depends upon two factors. First, with constant OG/OP ratio the rate of growth of the gold stock determines the rate of growth of the stock of COs. In Figure 6 this dependence is shown by the fact that the two lines labelled gold and currency obligation potential, $OG/OP = $ constant, are parallel on the semi-log graph. Between time t_0 and t_1 both stocks are assumed to grow at the rate r_0 (equal to the slope of the lines), between t_1 and t_4 they are assumed to grow at r_1, where $r_0 > r_1$.

Second, for any given growth rate in the stock of gold, the rate of growth of the currency obligation potential depends on the ratio OG/OP. Thus in Figure 6 the uppermost solid line segment between point t_1 and t_4 shows the currency obligations potential continue growing at r_0 even though the gold stock grows only at r_1. This is achieved by a constant fall in the OG/OP ratio, which in the graph is shown to be from 0.25 at t_1 to 0.20 at t_4. (The line DD will be explained below.)

In the context of the theoretical model of an optimum world monetary order, presented in Part One, the gold exchange standard achieves optimality through appropriate increases in the supply of international reserves. Whatever the rate of increase in the stock of gold or whatever its size at any given moment in time, the Banker's liquidity ratio can be chosen to attain the required quantity of reserves.

The currency obligations are held by the Other countries since they are readily exchangeable into gold, acceptable by others as money and bear interest. They are thus, in every essential respect, as good as gold and are superior to it in the sense that they yield a return and there is no need to guard a physical stock, since the CO certificates are useless to private individuals.

The preceding theoretical model permitted the analysis

to be focused on some important relationships. However, to keep it simple it was assumed that Other countries held only Banker's currency obligations. It is easy to modify the model by considering the possibility that Other countries wish to maintain a certain fraction of their international assets in the form of gold. If this is so, two major consequences follow. First, the degree of gold economizing inherent in the gold exchange standard is smaller than it is otherwise, and with a given ratio of gold to currency obligations maintained by Banker. Second, unless Other countries agree firmly to maintain a fixed ratio of gold to COs, the system can become unstable whenever Banker's solvency becomes suspect. Countries then begin to convert COs into gold and produce what is equivalent to a 'run on the bank'. This possibility and its relationship to some other features of the system will be discussed below.

History and Shortcomings of the System

The theoretical model just presented is an idealization of the basic idea of how the world could economize on the existing stock of gold. However, between this theoretical ideal and the real world there have been, and continue to be, great differences which can best be discussed in the context of actual past events.

The gold exchange standard has never been based on an explicit agreement among nations but, as has been mentioned before, represents the outcome of historic evolution. Thus, even during the hey-day of the gold standard before 1914, some central banks held national currencies as international reserves. In 1885 the central banks of Denmark, Norway and Sweden were authorized to hold balances with each other and to count these balances as reserves on which the issue of notes was based. In 1894, Russia began to hold some of its reserves in Berlin and other places. According to Nurkse (1944), in

1913 fifteen European central banks together held about 12 per cent of their total reserves in the form of foreign exchange.

In 1922, the Genoa Conference met to consider problems of reconstructing a viable international financial system after the turmoil created by the First World War. One of the problems confronting the Conference was that as a result of the general rise in prices and the retention of the old price of gold, the metal's production had declined by one-third, and the value of the existing stock had become a smaller fraction of world output and trade than it had been before the war. For this reason, the Conference recommended the adoption of a Gold Exchange Standard to economize on the use of existing stock and future output of gold.

While official agreement on the implementation of the recommendations was never achieved, the basic ideas nevertheless had considerable influence. Most major countries in the world subsequently adopted the legislation permitting their central banks to hold gold and foreign assets exchangeable into gold, some without and some with limitations on the fractions of reserves that had to consist of gold. After advantage had been taken of these laws, foreign exchange in 1927 and 1928 represented as much as 42 per cent of twenty-five major countries' total reserves, and ranged around 19 to 27 per cent during the periods 1924–6 and 1929–31. From the point of view of economizing on gold the system, therefore, was quite successful for a number of years.

However, by 1932 foreign exchange in the international portfolio assets of the twenty-four countries had fallen to 8 per cent and thereafter fell even further. The events leading up to this demise of the standard show quite clearly the importance that must be attached to the absence of a formal agreement on its operation. Thus, in 1926 France initiated strict domestic measures to restore confidence in the French franc. The external value of the franc was stabilized at a level which represented a significant undervaluation. As a consequence, France began to run balance of payments surpluses and to accumulate a very large stock of reserve assets, at first almost completely in the form of foreign exchange. However, a law passed in June 1928, prohibited the French central bank from acquiring any more foreign exchange. In 1931 France began to convert the previously acquired foreign exchange holdings into gold. By that time the world-wide depression had caused Great Britain to be in serious balance-of-payments difficulties. The French conversion of sterling holdings into gold added significantly to the pressures and probably was a major contributory cause to Britain's suspension of convertibility of the pound into gold. Since most central banks were required to hold foreign exchange convertible into gold, the sterling's inconvertibility forced them to dispose of their holdings of that currency, further aggravating the crisis. During the same period large quantities of dollar holdings also were exchanged into gold. These events caused the extinction of large sums of international reserves, since the pound and the dollar had been the most important reserve currencies.

The main reasons for this observed desire to convert foreign exchange assets into gold were two-fold. First, countries believed that their national prestige was enhanced if their currencies served as reserves for other nations, and they were thus members of the glamorous group of countries serving as World Bankers. In order to qualify for this role, currencies had to be freely convertible into gold, which in turn necessitated maintenance of a substantial share of total reserves in the form of gold. Consequently, those countries that wanted to have their currencies qualify as international reserves began converting some of their own assets into gold, and in the process reduced the entire system's effective economizing on the metal and created an unhealthy competition for the existing stock.

Second, according to the theoretical model of the gold

exchange standard presented above, the real economic incentive for holding foreign currencies rather than gold is that the former has a positive yield as compared with the zero yield on the latter. During the depression of the thirties, competitive devaluations of national currencies in relation to gold had the effect of endowing gold with capital value gains and a resultant positive rate of return, which tended to exceed that available in foreign currencies. Moreover, the frequent devaluations made the value of foreign currencies uncertain and reduced their usefulness as international reserves. Because of this capital value uncertainty, and the changes in the relative rates of return on gold and currency holdings, many countries switched their reserves from currencies into gold.

Analytically, these events, and the causes leading up to them, were due to the absence of any formal agreement among the countries of the world as to, first, which ones would serve as Bankers, second, that Others would keep down their gold holdings, and third, that Bankers' exchange rates in terms of gold must never be changed. If agreement on these matters had existed, the gold exchange standard might well have worked.

The developments after the Second World War led again to the establishment of a gold exchange standard and its history re-emphasizes that this form of international monetary order requires as a necessary, though by no means a sufficient condition, sound international co-operation.

The composition of international reserves held by all countries in the world outside of the Communist block is shown in Table 1. As can be seen, the share of gold in the total fell steadily from a high of 70·2 per cent in 1950 to a low of 51·4 per cent in 1968. On the other hand, international reserves in the form of foreign exchange, mainly U.S. Dollars and U.K. sterling, represented 26·4 per cent in 1950 and rose to 39·6 per cent in 1968. International reserves provided by the International Monetary Fund have remained a relatively insignificant part of the total, in spite of the fact that between 1954 and 1968 they increased from 3·2 per cent to 9·0 per cent of all international reserves.

As so many human institutions, the International Monetary Fund (I.M.F.), set up at Bretton Woods on the eve of the Second World War, was essentially designed to deal with the problems of the past. The rules guiding the relations among member states were set up to prevent the repetition of conditions which had haunted international economic relations during the thirties: competitive devaluations, discrimination in foreign exchange dealings and tariffs, lack of convertibility and disorderly capital flows. The I.M.F. was quite successful in achieving these objectives. However, the organization's provision of international reserves was totally inadequate. While the national ownership of freely spendable assets provided by the I.M.F. under a quota system was raised twice in twenty-five years, it remained only a small part of total international reserves, as can be seen from Table 1. Credits extended by the I.M.F. to members in balance-of-payments difficulties served in some measure as substitutes for owned reserves, but never became a significant share of total instruments available to countries for the settlement of debts.

In the absence of an orderly provision of reserves by international agreements, the world developed a temporarily very successful gold exchange standard almost by accident. The United States emerged from the Second World War with an overwhelmingly dominant economy in terms of productive capacity and national wealth, including reserves of monetary gold. In the eyes of the rest of the world dollar holdings were more desirable than gold, since they were readily exchangeable into the metal and brought interest to their holders. During the 1950s U.S. balance-of-payments deficits were welcomed as a source from which the reconstructed nations of Western Europe could replenish their depleted stocks of international reserves. They did so, holding mostly

Table 1

World Composition and Levels of International Reserves

Billions of U.S. Dollars

End of year	Total	Gold	Foreign exchange	Fund positions
1968[1]	73·5	37·8	29·1	6·6
1966	71·7	40·9	24·6	6·2
1964	69·9	40·8	23·7	5·4
1962	63·1	39·3	19·9	3·9
1960	60·2	38·0	18·6	3·6
1958	57·6	38·0	17·0	2·6
1956	58·2	38·1	17·8	2·3
1954	55·4	36·9	16·7	1·8
1952	51·8	35·8	14·2	1·8
1950	50·3	35·3	13·3	1·7
1948	49·5	34·5	13·4	1·6

Percentages

Year	Total	Gold	Foreign exchange	Fund positions
1968[1]	100·0	51·4	39·6	9·0
1966	100·0	57·0	34·3	8·6
1964	100·0	58·3	33·9	7·7
1962	100·0	62·3	31·5	6·2
1960	100·0	63·1	30·9	6·0
1958	100·0	66·0	29·5	4·5
1956	100·0	65·5	30·6	4·0
1954	100·0	66·7	30·1	3·2
1952	100·0	69·1	27·4	3·5
1950	100·0	70·2	26·4	3·4
1948	100·0	69·7	27·1	3·2

1. End of first quarter.

Source: *International Financial Statistics*, vol. 21, number 9, September 1968 for years 1958–68; *International Financial Statistics*, supplement to 1966–7 issues, for years 1948–56.

Notes: Foreign exchange holdings are bank deposits, Treasury bills, government securities and similar items denominated in convertible foreign currencies held by central banks, currency boards or other government agencies. Reserve position in the Fund are the amounts that a member, when experiencing a balance-of-payments deficit, may draw essentially automatically under the Fund's Gold Tranche policy. Total reserves were added from components of gold, foreign exchange and Fund positions given in source since total reserves given in same source did not add up exactly for some unknown reason. Total given in source differed by not more than $2 billion.

dollars but also exchanging some of them for gold, thus reducing the U.S. gold stock. It has been argued and it is probably correct that these deficits made possible the widespread return to convertibility in 1958 and that they made a significant contribution to world prosperity after 1950. The United States had thus, without formal international agreement, taken on the role of a World Banker and helped sustain an efficient monetary system.

The United Kingdom emerged from the Second World War reduced in relative economic and military power, but still at the heart of a Commonwealth and with the tradition and know-how of a World Banker. Because of sterling assets held by Commonwealth members and the facilities provided by London's private financial intermediaries the United Kingdom's national obligations served as international reserves to some extent, though they never were very significant and tended to become less so as Commonwealth ties were loosened during the fifties and sixties.

In 1960 Professor Robert Triffin published a now famous book in which he analysed the characteristics of a world monetary system based on reserves in the form of gold and national obligations. Showing that the U.S. stock of monetary gold grew at a slower rate than her stock of dollar obligations (it actually fell), he predicted a crisis of confidence in Banker's liquidity. This crisis promptly occurred later in 1960 when for the first time since the thirties, the value of U.S. short-term obligations exceeded the value of U.S. gold holdings. It manifested itself through speculative private sales of dollars and some official demand for gold for dollars in expectation of a devaluation.

The historic development of the liquidity positions of the United States and the United Kingdom are shown in Table 2. The United States experienced a steady decrease in her holdings of international reserves and an equally steady increase in external liquid liabilities, nearly all of which were to foreign official monetary authorities. The simultaneous rise in liabilities and decrease in assets resulted in a sharp fall of the ratio of reserves over assets,

Table 2

External Assets and Liabilities of the United States and the United Kingdom

Billions of U.S. Dollars

United States

End of year	(1) International reserves	(2) External liquid liab.	(3) $\frac{(1)}{(2)} \times 100$
1967	14·8	33·2	0·45
1966	14·9	29·8	0·50
1965	15·5	29·1	0·53
1964	16·7	29·0	0·58
1963	16·8	26·3	0·64
1962	17·2	24·1	0·71
1961	18·8	22·9	0·82
1960	19·4	21·0	0·92
1959	21·5	19·4	1·11
1958	22·5	16·8	1·34
1957	24·8	15·8	1·57
1956	23·7	14·9	1·59
1955	22·8	13·5	1·69
1954	23·0	12·5	1·84
1953	23·5	11·4	2·06
1952	24·7	10·4	2·38
1951	24·3	8·9	2·73
1950	24·3	8·9	2·73

Billions of U.S. Dollars

United Kingdom

End of year	(1) International reserves	(2) External liquid liab.	(3) $\frac{(1)}{(2)} \times 100$
1967	2·7	11·8	0·23
1966	3·1	12·5	0·25
1965	3·0	11·9	0·25
1964	2·3	11·8	0·20
1963	3·1	11·4	0·27
1962	3·3	10·7	0·31
1961	3·3	9·9	0·33
1960	3·7	10·9	0·34
1959	2·8	9·8	0·29
1958	3·1	9·4	0·33
1957	2·4	9·2	0·26
1956	2·3	9·6	0·24
1955	2·4	10·0	0·24
1954	3·0	10·4	0·29
1953	2·7	9·8	0·28
1952	2·0	9·0	0·22
1951	2·4	10·0	0·24
1950	3·4	9·8	0·35

Sources: *International Financial Statistics*, vol. 21, number 9, September 1968 for years 1961–68; *International Financial Statistics*, supplement to 1967–68 Issues, for years 1950–60.

Notes: International Reserves are the figures taken from row one of the I.F.S. country tables. They comprise gold, foreign exchange and the gold tranche positions of the monetary authorities. External liquid liabilities are taken from row four of the I.F.S. country tables. They represent the liquid liabilities of the government to foreign monetary institutions, banks and international agencies.

from 2·73 in 1950 to 0·45 in 1967. The ratio fell below one for the first time in 1960, the year of the first dollar-crisis.

While the U.S. time series are characterized by steady and pronounced trends, the British series exhibit very little trend, but substantial and persistent fluctuations. Also remarkable is the fact that the U.K. ratio of assets to liabilities has been much lower than the U.S. ratio throughout the period, averaging about one half of the lowest ratio attained by the United States in 1967. Because of the low initial ratio very little growth in external liabilities, i.e. international reserves in the form of pound sterling, took place during the period.

Figure 6 above lends itself well to a somewhat abstract but, nevertheless, useful explanation of the events during the fifties. The line labelled D D shows the world demand for dollars which is equal to the supply actually made available by U.S. deficits. It is shown to grow at a faster rate than the Currency Obligation Potential, which in the theoretical world of the gold exchange standard, presented in the first part of this chapter, is determined by the rate of growth in the gold stock and the ratio of gold to obligations considered necessary by the 'depositors'. Between period t_0 and t_2 no problem arose since U.S. gold reserves exceeded U.S. obligations by a margin considered safe by the holders of the dollars. However, at period t_2 (1960?) depositors became alarmed, and started the 'run' on the Bank because the ratio of Banker's obligations to gold had begun to exceed the 'safe' level.

At that time the leaders of the western world realized that the gold exchange standard needed to be improved by official agreements, and that it was necessary to accept a decrease in Banker's ratio of gold to demand obligations. An assumed acceptable rate of decrease in this ratio is shown in Figure 6 by the relationship between the uppermost solid line, and the line labelled gold after t_1. At the same time, however, diplomatic pressure was brought to bear in the United States to decrease the rate at which the actual supply of her obligations grew in the future. For a number of reasons, the United States was unable to reduce the balance of payments deficit, and after time t_3, dollar obligations relative to gold again began to exceed those considered prudent for a Banker. In 1967 private speculation against the dollar once more became rampant.

This highly stylized description of the U.S. experience as the World Banker brings out the basic dilemma inherent in the gold exchange standard: since gold is the ultimate standard of value, its value relative to the Banker's currency must never be changed. With the price of gold thus fixed, only by coincidence does its supply grow at the same rate as the welfare maximizing demand for reserves. Consequently, countries holding Banker's obligations must be willing to accept changes, and historically they have been mostly decreases, in the Banker's liquidity position.

International agreements formalizing this willingness have been difficult to reach in practice, since there always appears to be at least one maverick non-cooperating nation which finds such agreements contrary to her own national interests and sabotages them through hoarding of gold and other means.

However, even if such agreements on the Banker's liquidity position could be reached among the governments of the world, the gold exchange standard has several other glaring weaknesses. First, private holders of national currency obligations may not be convinced that Banker has a sound liquidity position, even if their governments are. With the price of gold fixed in the downward direction through the basic setup of the system, switches from national currency obligations into gold are safe and relatively cheap. Periodic private speculation against the dollar and sterling has taken place in the past, in spite of strong co-operation among central banks, and it can be expected to take place in future. Such speculation causes shifts of private capital, delays or speedups in commercial purchases and deliveries, changes in exchange rates and in general has unsettling and harmful effects on world trade, capital flows and welfare.

Second, the growth in total international reserves depends on Banker's balance-of-payments deficits. At present and for the foreseeable future, governments do not seem to be able to set the size of their balance-of-payments deficits with precision. Consequently, the actual growth in reserves is likely to be erratic, unpredictable and unrelated to need, probably adding to world instability, because Banker and Other countries are unable to regulate their balance of payments in the necessary optimum fashions.

Third, the Banker nation surrenders the right to use devaluation as a policy instrument in the quest for domestic stability, full employment, growth and balance-of-payments deficits of the required size. Since at least 1960, United States economic policy making has been severely constrained by an allegedly excessive balance-of-payments deficit that could not be rectified by devaluation. As a result the United States had to impose measures to reduce imports and capital outflows, and to set high interest rates conflicting with the objective of increased domestic economic growth.

However, a co-operation among countries of a kind somewhat different from those discussed above can eliminate this constraint on the Banker's policies. It is known that if there are two countries, one's surplus is the other's deficit and vice versa. Consequently, if one country's international payments are balanced, so are those of the other. Similarly, the sum of all imbalances of $n - 1$ countries is equal to the imbalance of the nth country. From this relationship arises the possibility that the size of Banker's external deficit can be determined by the appropriate exchange rate and interest rate adjustments by all the other countries. In practice, the United States has been unable to make other industrial countries take appropriate actions to free her of the need for balance-of-payments adjustments.

Moreover, the question might be raised whether the costs of such co-operation do not exceed the benefits derived from it. It requires that Other countries agree, through political bargaining, on which should do the adjusting by how much and how frequently. It is not clear that the resultant frequency and size of exchange rate adjustments are optimum from the point of view of maximizing world trade and capital flows.

Fourth, related to the two preceding points is the difficulty that, under the system, some human beings have to determine what the desired rate of increase in the supply of reserves should be in the future. Such judgements are not only technically very difficult to make because of the uncertainties surrounding the timing and magnitude of business cycles, rates of growth, etc., but they also involve intercountry comparisons of utility since the rate of reserve growth has effects on world-wide rates of inflation, and price increases are disliked by countries in differing degrees. The resultant need for political bargaining and possible delays in decisions have been discussed above.

Fifth, under the gold exchange standard the world's richest economy is the most likely candidate for the role of the World Banker. Successful operation of the scheme assures that Banker receives a regular flow of resources called 'seigniorage', by analogy to the resources which used to accrue to sovereign rulers of the past who had the right to mint coin with a face value larger than the intrinsic metal value in the coin and the cost of manufacturing, etc. This seigniorage accrues to Banker because the only way the rest of the world can acquire Banker's national obligations is by running a balance-of-payments surplus, thus transferring real resources or claims on assets to him. However, just as in the case of gold coins the value of the seigniorage is not equal to the face value of the coins, so the nominal value of the resources accruing to Banker has to be adjusted for various 'costs' to arrive at an estimate of the value of the seigniorage.

The present value of the seigniorage acquired in one year can be determined as follows. Assume that there are interest payments on Banker's obligations at the annual rate r, costs of running the business equal to c per cent per annum on deposits, and that Banker can place the acquired resources in the open market at an annual rate R, which is equal to the marginal productivity of capital. Discounting the future annual payments at the social discount rate of d, the present value of seigniorage (S) due to one year's deficit (D) is

$$S = \left[\frac{R-r-c}{(1+d)} + \frac{R-r-c}{(1+d)^2} + \frac{R-r-c}{(1+d)^3} + \ldots + \frac{R-r-c}{(1+d)^n} \right] \times D$$

where n is the year at which the Banker's currency obligation is traded in by running a balance of payments surplus with the rest of the world. If n approaches infinity, present value becomes $[(R-r-c)/d] \times D$. As can be seen from this formula, assuming $r = 0$, $c = 0$ and $R = d$ makes the value of seigniorage equal to the deficit D.

A calculation of the benefits to the United States or the United Kingdom of being the World Banker in practice is quite complicated, since it is difficult to determine the costs associated with the role, especially how big gold reserves would have been if the country had not served as the Banker, when the resources have to be repaid, and what rate of interest is paid on outstanding obligations. However, it may be worth noting that the total obligations of the United States held by foreign official institutions was valued at $16 billion in the fall of 1967, while those of the United Kingdom were £2 billion before the November 1967 devaluation. Under the assumption that $R = 10$ per cent and $(r + c) = 5$ per cent, then these obligations resulted in a flow of resources valued at $800 million to the United States, and £100 million to the United Kingdom during the year 1967. Moreover, since Banker's currency is widely used as a means of payment in private transactions of international trade and finance, private foreigners tend to keep quantities of this country's currency as transactions balances, which in turn are a source of seigniorage in the same way as the officially held balances. Moreover, the World Banker also sells other banking and kindred services to international business clients, such as insurance and brokerage, which are a source of comparative advantage and gainful use of resources.

However, this last group of added advantages should not be attributed to being the World Banker, since causation probably runs the other way: a country dominating world trade and finance through its relative size, financial and industrial development logically grows into the role of issuing currency obligations acceptable to governments as official reserves. Certainly, the United States and Great Britain were the dominant trading nations long before becoming World Bankers.

The phenomenon of seigniorage thus is the main source of a transfer of real resources from the poorer to the richest nations of the world. Such a redistribution of income is neither efficient nor equitable and must be considered as being an undesirable by-product of the gold exchange standard.

Sixth, gold retains a central role in the operation of the system. Banker continues to purchase all gold offered in the free market at a fixed price. From a social point of view, the process involved is that resources of labour and capital are used in some areas of the world to mine and refine gold. More resources are used to re-bury and guard it at the Banker's central depositories, such as the New York Federal Reserve Bank and Fort Knox in the United States. Such a process tends to be socially wasteful, as has been recognized by most national governments which over the last few decades have severed previously existing ties between their fiat money supplies and gold. Logically, such a severance would also be possible for the gold exchange standard because if agreement on the working of the system were perfect and reliable, Banker would never have to exchange his national currency obligations into gold. However, if such a break with gold were to be made, the essence of the gold exchange standard would be destroyed and the emergent systems would fall into the analytical category of schemes known as *centrally created reserves*, which will be discussed in the next chapter.

Lastly, the gold exchange standard contains no effective and equitable method for assuring adjustment to balance-of-payments disequilibria. Under the gold standard adjustment is automatic through the effects gold movements have on money supplies. Freely fluctuating exchange rates carry directly all burden of adjustment to disequilibrating disturbances. Under the gold exchange standard, when Other countries incur deficits, they sooner or later feel the discipline of running out of reserves so that real adjustments are forced upon them. But when the Banker runs deficits excessive in the light of the world's demand for its obligations as reserves, adjustment pressures of the normal kind are lacking. Yet, these Banker deficits are excessive by definition and force hardships upon the countries at whose expense they occur. Efficiency and equity might demand that at least part of the necessary adjustment to the imbalances be undertaken by the Banker. Moreover, also among Other countries there is no effective adjustment mechanism working on the surplus countries. During the 1950s, for example, Germany and the Netherlands ran substantial and consistent balance of payments surpluses the elimination of which would have required exceedingly severe deflation by the other major industrial countries of the West. Only after many years of surpluses did the diplomatic pressures of the deficit countries force Germany and the Netherlands into an upward revaluation of their currencies.

In spite of the success of diplomatic pressures in this episode and the general development of unwritten 'rules of the game' allegedly guiding the behaviour of countries with imbalances in their external accounts, the absence of any compelling method by which the burden of adjustment is put on Banker and Other surplus, as well as deficit countries, must be considered to be a serious disadvantage of the gold exchange standard.

Proposals for Reform of the Gold Exchange Standard

Following the 1960 dollar crisis and Triffin's diagnosis of the world monetary system's ills, scholars, central bankers and bankers such as Edward Bernstein (1963), Per Jacobson (1962), Friedrich Lutz (1963), S. Posthuma (1963), Robert Roosa (1962), Henry Wallich (1961) and Xenophon Zolotas (1961 and 1962) published treatises containing their own diagnosis of the problem and prescriptions towards its solution.

Most of these writers saw the short-run solution of the issues of the times in increased international co-operation, as is well exemplified by the title of H. Wallich's (1961) paper, 'Co-operation to solve the Gold Problem'. The many areas in which strong co-operation is needed to make the gold exchange standard work have been discussed above. They include consultation on the consistency of national economic policies, the sharing of the adjustment burden and the granting of mutual credits, especially to the United States as the World Banker. The latter step can be interpreted as an agreement to accept a lower Banker's liquidity ratio. However, some of these analysts considered such co-operation agreements as being insufficient and they demanded that the United States strengthen the existing system by granting gold guarantees on the dollar balances held by foreign governments. It is interesting to note that this proposal was not supported by American experts. However, R. Roosa, who at the time was Under Secretary of the U.S. Treasury for International Monetary Affairs, argued for, and was able to introduce, the practice whereby the United States sold to foreign governments bonds denominated in their own currencies. These bonds, known as Roosa bonds, provided the equivalent of a gold guarantee to countries which chose not to devalue their currencies in case the United

States did so, but provided only a guarantee of fixed value in national currency for those which kept their exchange rates pegged to the dollar. These bonds never became a large share of U.S. obligations. In general, the system was well able to deal with the short-run problems after many of the experts' recommendations for co-operation had been put into effect.

While there was rather broad agreement on the short-run solution to the crisis of confidence, two broad proposals were made to solve the problem of supplying world liquidity in the long-run. These proposals were made in recognition of the fact that the supply of liquidity for nearly a decade had depended on U.S. deficits and threatened to dry up once the U.S. balance-of-payments deficit was eliminated. The characteristic common to the proposals discussed here is that they sought the solution within the framework of the existing institutional set-up.

The first set of proposals concerned the systematic use of more national currencies as international reserves. Thus, if and when the United States began to run a balance-of-payments surplus, the stock of outstanding dollar obligations should not be reduced, but instead the United States should begin to hold other foreign currencies. This practice would assure a growth in total world reserves and facilitate the adjustment problems of deficit countries. The main difficulties with this solution are the same as those with the gold exchange standard with one or two Bankers. The rate of growth of world reserves depends on national balance-of-payments deficits. A country running large payments deficits makes available large supplies of its currency, but also reduces the attractiveness of its obligations as reserves. Furthermore, there exists the danger of frequent and unsettling shifts of previously accumulated reserves, away from weakening to strengthening currencies.

Most of the preceding shortcomings of the multiple currency reserve approach can be remedied by appropriate agreements and some of these were proposed. For example, gold guarantees on all currencies would make it unnecessary to be afraid of devaluations and the speculative shifts could be prevented. To even out short-run fluctuations in balance of payments and assure constant demand for all eligible currencies it had been proposed that all countries hold currencies and gold in specified proportions.

The preceding set of proposals for a multiple currency reserve system never were implemented. One reason for official coolness toward the plans may have been the recognition that they require such a large degree of international co-operation and agreement that they would be exceedingly difficult to negotiate. Moreover, if such agreement were attainable, it might better be used to put into effect a more fundamental reform of the system along the lines discussed in the next chapter.

The second broad approach to the long-run liquidity problem emphasized the potential role of the International Monetary Fund, through the creation of more owned reserves, especially the expansion of the quotas, of more credit facilities and generally greater willingness of countries to use the Fund's facilities. The main trouble with these proposals was that they fell short of granting the Fund the right to create internationally acceptable means of payment by fiat, since the unconditional drawing rights and conditional added credits would have to be repaid by the countries to which they were granted initially. Moreover, to attain some of the drawing rights, countries would have to surrender gold to the Fund.

Some of the proposals for modification of the I.M.F. made after 1960 were in fact implemented, such as an increase in quotas and the development of added credit facilities, the most important of which became known as the General Agreement to Borrow. These changes have strengthened the existing gold exchange standard, but public and official thinking about the future of the I.M.F. slowly moved towards acceptance of the notion that the world needs an authority which can create owned and non-extinguishable means of payment acceptable for settlement of debts among nations. It is difficult to pin-point the precise time of the idea's intellectual victory. However, it is an historic fact that at the September 1967 meetings of the International Monetary Fund in Rio de Janeiro, the Board of Governors approved the outline of a scheme for the creation of fiat reserves. Only history can tell whether this act signalled the end of the gold exchange standard and the beginning of a new era.

8 Centrally Created Reserves

Historically the monetary sectors in the industrialized economies of the West have evolved from decentralization and *laissez-faire* to centralization and strict control. This evolution was accompanied and caused by the growing recognition that the money supply is too important an element in economic growth and stability of nations to be left uncontrolled by man. If this historic evolution in national economies is a reliable guide to coming developments in the field of the international monetary sector, then the ultimate form of international monetary organization will be one resembling the U.S. Federal Reserve System, the Bank of England or any other national central banking system, with the world supply of reserves firmly in the conscious control of man.

In a sense the entire first part of this book is concerned with the reasons why the world needs a certain, controlled supply of international liquidity at levels at which world welfare is maximized. These reasons, which need not be repeated here, provide the justification for the establishment of such a supra-national bank. Its function is nearly identical to that of the national central banks in that it is to provide the community of nations with liquidity sufficient to enable the system's operation at maximum efficiency.

The most important difference between national monetary authorities as they are known today and an international central bank now envisioned is that the former is part of a complete government executive, with the power to tax and enforce its legislation, while the latter essentially is a voluntary association of nation states, with practically no effective power to oversee execution of its orders. The existence of this difference will be seen to be at the heart of many of the difficulties encountered in the negotiations for the establishment of a world monetary order based on a system of centrally created reserves.

While it is relatively simple to state these basic properties of the blueprint for such an order, it is considerably more difficult to present its institutional and operational details. The reasons for this difficulty are that theoretically there are many alternative methods for the creation, distribution and administration of these centrally created reserves, and that in practice many proposals have been made combining these theoretical alternatives into specific plans.

The following discussion presents the most fundamental institutional environment envisaged in common by all plans, and then turns to the theoretical alternative methods of, first, distributing seigniorage; second, deciding on how many reserves to create; third, keeping the fiat money convertible; fourth, maintaining a stable value of the fiat money; and fifth, assuring adjustment to balance-of-payments disequilibria. These topics of discussion have been chosen because they contain the keys to the essential differences between plans for international monetary order based on a supply of fiat money and because an understanding of the principles underlying each of the choices illuminates the fundamental working of this class of reform proposals. The special significance of each of the topics will become apparent as the discussion proceeds.

The Basic Environment

The basic institutional environment to which the international monetary system has to be fitted is the continued existence of independent nation states. One of the most important rights of these sovereign nations is the making of economic policy through regulation of the money supply, exchange rates, and fiscal policy, whose existence must be recognized explicitly by all reform plans based on a central reserve creating agency, and imposes two important limitations on a world monetary authority.

First, the 'money' issued will not be circulating publicly. Day-to-day private transactions of international trade and finance will continue to be executed in national currencies. The centrally created international money will be used only by national governments in the settlement of debts arising among themselves as a result of official intervention in the foreign exchange markets. It has been discussed in chapter 2 above how the pegging of exchange rates can give rise to these intergovernmental debts in a welfare maximizing world monetary order.

Second, whereas national central banks can regulate the quantity of money in the economies over which they have jurisdiction by influencing the quantity of the banking system's reserve assets, the discount rate and the fractional reserve requirements, the international agency has no such powers to regulate total liquidity in the world, primarily because national governments continue to be free to set the levels of their money supplies for purposes of domestic stability and with only little regard to their level of international reserves. Therefore, the total quantity of money *privately* used in the world through its effects on monetary rates of interest, has an important influence on national and average world-wide employment and prices and is not under the control of the international agency.

None of the plans for international monetary order to be analysed below envisage the extinction, or even significant reduction, of national monetary sovereignty. However the establishment and operation of a central international monetary agency, even on the limited basis just described, implies the surrender of some economic sovereignty and the close co-operation among nations. Moreover, it is likely that the experience of working together, bargaining and communicating provided by such an international organization will make its own contribution towards greater understanding and trust, thus paving the way for future increased co-operation and surrender of sovereignty. However, such developments are speculative and all plans for a new international monetary order proceed from the assumption that it will serve a voluntary association of independent nation states.

The Distribution of Social Seigniorage

In the preceding chapter 'seigniorage' was defined as the value of resources accruing to the issuer of money as a result of the fact that the face value of the money issued exceeded the cost of producing and servicing it.

In the present chapter the concept of 'social seigniorage' is introduced and is defined as the social savings of resources realized by the switch from commodity to fiat money. More precisely, the present value of social seigniorage (SS) arising from the issue of D units of paper money over a given time period is equal to

$$SS = \left[\frac{R-c}{1+d} + \frac{R-c}{(1+d)^2} + \frac{R-c}{(1+d)^3} + \cdots + \frac{R-c}{(1+d)^n} \right] \times D$$

where n is the period at which the paper money has to be 'cashed in' or is replaced by a commodity substitute, R is the marginal social productivity of the resources D which would have been required to produce commodity money of equal value, c is the social unit cost of servicing the fiat money, such as printing and replacing worn out paper money, policing against counterfeitting and provision of check clearing services, and d is the social rate of discount. Assuming constancy of R, c and d throughout the life of the fiat money, and assuming that life to approach infinity, the present value of social seigniorage from the issuance of D units of paper money is

$$SS = \left[\frac{R-c}{d} \right] \times D$$

Thus, if c is zero and $R = d$, the value of the social seigniorage is equal to the face value of the money issued.

It should be noted that the present value of seigniorage accruing to the issuer of money was found to be

$$S = \left[\frac{R-r-c}{d}\right] \times D$$

under the assumption of an infinite life of the money and where r is the interest rate paid to the holders of the money. Thus, it is seen that the essential difference between the two concepts is found in the term r. As will be shown below, the payment of interest to money holders is one of the methods for the distribution of social seigniorage away from the issuer of the money to those who hold it.

The potential value of social seigniorage arising from the issuance of an international fiat money is substantial. Assuming, for example, that the world stock of international reserves was $70 billion at the end of 1968, then an increase of reserves of 3 per cent in the year 1969, represents a potential value of $2·1 billion. At a growth rate of 3 per cent per year, the stock of international reserves would be $180 billion at the end of the year 2000. During the year 2001 the potential social seigniorage is valued at $5·4 billion. The cost of servicing the international fiat money is very near to zero so that, under the reasonable assumptions that the social rate of discount is equal to the marginal social productivity of resources, the true value of the social seigniorage, relevant for the present discussion of distribution, is approximately equal to the potential value calculated above.

It is of considerable significance for the welfare of nations what formula for the distribution of this social seigniorage is adopted by the international institution charged with issuing the world fiat reserves, since it involves the availability of valuable resources which can be employed for raising living standards directly through higher consumption levels or indirectly through capital formation.

Logically, there exist three basic methods for the

distribution of social seigniorage, each of which has been embodied in a class of reform-proposals made in recent years. The three methods of distribution for convenience will be called the central government, the free market and the transactions demand methods and will be discussed next with the reform proposals based on them.

Central Government Method

National monetary authorities never face any 'problem' in connexion with the distribution of social seigniorage even though it is substantial as growing economies are supplied with large quantities of needed paper money. In the United States, for example, the cumulative total value of seigniorage from the issuance of paper money alone was $40 billion at the end of 1967, assuming that the cost of the money's production and maintenance have been zero in the past and will continue to be so in the future. In recent years the seigniorage has been about $2·5 billion per annum.

The seigniorage accruing to national monetary authorities rarely gives rise to any discussion because the creation of money is part of the central government activity and, as such, the excess of the face value of the paper money over its cost of production and administration goes directly into the general revenue of the Treasury. In the United States, for example, the mints responsible for producing currency are an administrative division of the Treasury and 'profits' from their operation enter government revenue directly. From there this seigniorage is distributed to society as a whole by the purchase of public goods or through the redistribution of income. The process of distribution can best be understood by realizing that in theory government expenditures for public goods and income redistribution are determined by society's needs and available alternative resource uses, while taxation rates are set to raise revenue sufficient to meet the cost of these expenditures. The existence of seigniorage permits these tax rates to be lower than they otherwise would have to be.

Another way of looking at the process of seigniorage distribution by national governments is to consider that the newly issued money each year permits the government to purchase certain quantities of goods and services with 'cash', which it did not obtain through taxation, and which does not add to the rate of price increase existing otherwise, since the public needs this cash to carry on business activity at the new level reached during the year.

The purchase of world public goods, or the redistribution of world income with the seigniorage from the issue of international reserve assets has been proposed by Sir Maxwell Stamp (1962). In his plan he proposed that the seigniorage from world liquidity creation be channelled to the less developed countries. Such an objective can easily be attained by issuance of the agreed upon quantity of reserve assets to the less developed countries, which would then spend them on real resources in the developed countries. By agreement the latter countries would accept these assets and treat them as reserves. The resultant flow of resources from developed to less developed countries would not have to be reversed as long as the developed countries continued to abide by the agreements setting up the monetary order and economic conditions did not call for a decrease in average holdings of reserves.

Pursuing the logic of Stamp's basic idea, it follows that, after the disappearance of the less developed countries' need for capital, seigniorage could be used to support other world-wide programmes of income redistribution as appear desirable at the time. Or alternatively seigniorage could be spent directly on world public goods and services, as for example, a supranational peace keeping force, international courts of law, the maintenance of agencies regulating and maintaining international air, land and sea ways, collecting and interpreting statistics in economics, demography and meteorology.

The most important objection to this plan for the

disposal of social seigniorage from world liquidity creation is that the method is inconsistent with the current wave of nationalism since it obliges the developed countries to surrender resources without commensurate compensation. The developed countries prefer to have foreign aid under the control of national governments where it can be made to serve the national interest and to have the world fiat money with seigniorage distributed some other way. Moreover, the idea of a centrally directed scheme for the redistribution of income and the purchase of public goods presupposes a degree of international co-operation much stronger than that required to achieve agreement on fiat money creation with some other methods of seigniorage distribution. Linking up liquidity creation and public expenditures thus tends to postpone attainment of the former until political conditions are ripe for the latter.

A variant of the central government method of distributing seigniorage has been proposed in a joint paper by Albert Hart, Nicholas Kaldor and Jan Tinbergen (1964). The plan revives the old idea of having monetary assets 'backed' by a number of staple commodities, such as grains, cotton and metals in proportions dependent upon relative scarcities. The main objective of the plan is to aid the less developed countries through creating additional demand for the products in whose production they are specialized, raising world prices for these commodities and turning the terms of trade in favour of the producing countries. The alleged advantages of this type of resource transfer to the less developed countries are that the aid loses the odium of 'charity' now attached to it, and that the expanded demand provides a stimulus to economic development through Keynesian type employment, and Hirschman-type linkage effects.

The objection to this plan is simply its wastefulness, since it uses up all of the potential social seigniorage in the process of acquiring and maintaining a stock of commodities. In terms of the preceding analysis of social seigniorage the effect of the plan would be to make $R = c$ and

$SS = 0$. For example, assuming world reserves were \$67 billion at the end of 1967, the value of socially useful commodities withdrawn from circulation and stored for ever would be \$2 billion in 1968 if reserves were made to grow at 3 per cent. In the year 2000 the annual withdrawal of resources would be \$6·8 billion under the assumption of a 3·5 per cent growth rate in reserves. That year the stock of commodities backing world liquidity would be worth \$161 billion, and if the cost of storing, guarding and maintaining this merchandise is conservatively assumed to be 6 per cent of the stock's value per year it would become a significant additional burden valued at \$9·7 billion. Thus, while under a genuine system of fiat money all of these resources could be made available to increase the world's standard of living, under the Hart–Kaldor–Tinbergen (1964) plan they would be used to increase and maintain a very large, sterile stock of commodities. It is highly unlikely that the increased welfare in the less developed countries resulting from the improved terms of trade and Hirschman-type linkage effects under the plan would be large enough to exceed the loss of potential welfare from the direct waste of the resources.

Free Market Method

Free market economies have developed substitutes for commodity money, the best known of which are the various forms of negotiable instruments, above all checks and demand deposits. In the process, the free market has solved automatically the 'problem' of distributing social seigniorage through the payment of interest.

The role of interest in the distribution of social seigniorage can be explained most easily by the following schematic sketch of the historic evolution of the banking business. Goldsmiths are alleged to have taken on the job of storing bullion for their customers, at first simply as a sideline to their regular business. They issued certificates of deposit to the owners of the gold, which began to circulate freely in place of the gold itself since every new owner was confident that he could obtain the metal whenever he needed it. Only rarely did special circumstances give rise to the actual conversion of certificates into the metal. The smarter goldsmiths eventually realized that it was quite safe to keep only a fraction of their deposits backed by gold and they began to convert a fraction of their gold deposits into income-yielding investments, such as securities, loans, houses, land, merchandise inventories, and machines.

The gold put back into circulation in this manner was redeposited with other goldsmiths and in turn was used to make more investments after an appropriate fraction had been retained for liquidity purposes. Ultimately the circulation of certificates exceeded the existing stock of gold by a multiple, the exact size of which was determined by the fraction of gold deposits retained as a liquidity reserve. How large a fraction of deposits needed to be retained depended on the stability of the demand deposits and the cost and availability of liquid secondary reserves, as is well-known from the theory of banking.

The first goldsmiths who made these productive investments with their customers' deposits earned extraordinarily high profits. However, in a free market such high profits attract new entries into the business and soon competition for these profitable deposits began to develop. The main forms in which this competition expressed itself were the provision of more services to depositors, as for example cheque-writing privileges, and the payment of interest. The costs of doing business and the interest payments tended to rise through competitive responses until in the end profits from the banking business were reduced to normal.

In terms of the preceding discussion of seigniorage the formal condition for competitive equilibrium is:

$$S = \left(\frac{R-r-c}{d}\right) \times D = 0$$

where S is the present value of seigniorage accruing to the issuer of D units of paper money, R is the yield on the investments made by the money-issuer, c is the cost of administering the business per unit of deposit, including a normal profit to the entrepreneur and his capital and d is the social rate of discount. From this equation it follows that the interest rate on deposits with the goldsmiths (r) is $r = R - c$. Since the marginal productivity of investments and the cost of carrying on the banking business are determined by technological conditions in the economy as a whole, the yield on deposits of money is seen to be determined by the same factors.

In this situation of competitive equilibrium, society still reaps benefits from social seigniorage due to the use of paper money in place of the gold. However, these benefits accrue to the holders of the money in the form of interest and services on their deposits and, consequently, in proportion to the extent to which they contributed to the demand for paper money and the generation of the social savings.

Of the major proposals for reform of the international monetary system made in recent years, only that by Triffin places emphasis on the role of interest. He argues that the payment of interest to the holders of centrally created reserves makes these assets more desirable than gold. According to his plan, the central authority would receive deposits of gold and national currencies in return for which it would issue the international fiat money. The national currencies thus received would be invested in the securities markets of member nations, yielding an interest income to the Bank at the rate R per unit of outstanding fiat money. Though Triffin does not discuss these issues explicitly, his bank would presumably pay interest to the holders of the money at a rate high enough so that the profits from these investments are zero after payment of operating costs (c). In terms of the preceding analytical framework, these conditions are equivalent to the condition $S = R - r - c = 0$.

The method of distributing the seigniorage through payment of interest to the money-holders has the disadvantage of requiring the central authority to manage a very large asset portfolio with all of the difficulties of judging credit worthiness of debtors, maintaining maturity structure of the portfolio, collecting and disbursing interest and dividends, etc. The investment decisions by a group of directors could mean doom or success to private entrepreneurs and governments, especially since the investments represent demand for a country's debt instruments and influence the level of national exchange rates. For these reasons political pressures on these directors would tend to be strong and, in general, their positions would represent an undesirable concentration of economic power. It would most likely be possible to routinize the portfolio management of the authority and leave little discretion and power to directors. However, such a system might prove to be quite inflexible and incapable of adjusting to changing conditions, aggravating cyclical instabilities and hindering secular adjustments in international trade and finance. Consequently, management by rule may be as undesirable as leaving too much discretionary power in the hands of the directors.

In spite of these objections, the free market method of distributing social seigniorage carries considerable intellectual appeal since it approximates the solution perfect competition would attain. However, chances for its adoption are not good, primarily because of the availability of a superior method of distributing seigniorage called the transactions demand method, which will be discussed next

Transactions Demand Method

The distribution of social seigniorage under the central government method and the Stamp Plan results in the ultimate transfer of resources between countries when the initial recipients of the newly created money spend it.

Thus, if the initial recipients could be required to hold on to it, no other countries in the world would be required to give up resources as a result of fiat money creation and distribution. But while 'money' that can never be spent is not really money and the preceding analysis is unrealistic, it dramatizes the point that it is the expenditure of paper money received free initially which gives rise to resource transfers and the 'problem' of social seigniorage distribution.

Analytically the permanent hoarding of the newly issued reserves is equal to the maintenance of an average balance of cash equal to the sum received. Thus, if countries are required to aim for a holding of average reserve balances just equal to the sum they were given from the fiat money-creating agency, the reserves would be available for purposes of meeting temporary balance of payments deficits and thus would serve the purposes for which they were created without causing intercountry resource transfers attributable to their creation and distribution. Periods of temporary shortage below the sum of fiat money received have to be met by periods of excess holdings above that sum and accounting of a country's position in this sense requires keeping a running total of reserve unit days in surplus and deficit.

If newly created reserves are distributed among nations so that each country receives only such quantities as it tends to hold on the average, the *creation* and *distribution* of reserves in this manner involves no intercountry transfer of resources and retains a theoretical neutrality of money in the allocation of resources.[1]

The concept of social seigniorage distribution according to these general principles was incorporated in both the White and Keynes plans, which served respectively as the U.S. and U.K. backed blueprints for the establishment of the International Monetary Fund after the Second World

1. This is strictly true only if interest adjustments are incorporated into the calculation of average reserve balance shortages and surpluses in order to reflect the fact that real resources acquired today in exchange for fiat money are worth more than these resources repayable in the future.

War. Under the I.M.F. charter the concept is reflected in the 'quotas', which determine the quantity of internationally acceptable assets, such as dollars, sterling, or gold a country may obtain in return for its own currency. These same quotas are proposed to serve as a basis for the distribution of Special Drawing Rights, the fiat money to be issued by the I.M.F., according to the agreement reached at the 1967 meetings of the International Monetary Fund in Rio de Janeiro, Brazil.

During the scholarly debate over world monetary reform in the late fifties and early sixties, proposals incorporating the same principles of distribution had been made by E. Bernstein (1963) who envisaged modification and expansion of the role of the International Monetary Fund through quota increases, and more liberal use of the resources available under the quota system. Modigliani and Kenen (1966) also proposed distribution of newly created assets on the basis of long-run demand, like the I.M.F. quotas R.. Roosa (1965) in his book on reform written after he had left his position as Assistant Secretary of Treasury for Monetary Affairs also suggested distribution of fiat money on the principle of average long run demand. However, Roosa introduced into his proposal the idea that depositors of national currency should pay modest interest to the I.M.F. in return for the internationally acceptable assets they obtain for their national currencies. This idea of a 'charge' for liquidity appears to be a sound banking principle but does in fact create the problem of how to distribute the potentially large interest receipts. The preceding analysis of seigniorage distribution has shown that these kinds of interest payments *by* rather than *to* depositors are inconsistent with the need for the efficient distribution of social seigniorage.

While all of these reform proposals agree on the general validity of the principle that newly created reserves should be distributed according to nations' long-run demand for them, disagreement exists as to the actual formulas to be used in the measurement of this demand. The analysis at the end of chapter 3 indicated the theoretical and statistical difficulties with the measurement. Moreover, since the formulas reflect both national prestige and real economic costs or benefits to individual countries, distribution formulas tend to be determined by political bargaining, where economic and military power tend to play a more important role than economic efficiency and a world welfare calculus.

Thus, White's proposed formula (see Gardner, 1956, and Harrod, 1951) for the computation of national quotas under the I.M.F. favoured the United States since it based the calculation of quotas on the level of gold holdings, national incomes and fluctuations and scale of international payments at the time when the United States position in these respects was extraordinarily strong. Keynes' (1943) formula, on the other hand, provided that the level of each country's exports and imports for the three years immediately before the war be used as a base. This formula would have been relatively favourable for the United Kingdom, because of the country's relatively strong position in the period just before the war. Ultimately, the I.M.F. Agreements provided for quotas based on the White plan, though the formula was not made part of the official document and political considerations appear to have modified somewhat the distribution resulting from the mechanical application of the formula alone. Since the initial quotas were agreed upon, the I.M.F. quotas of small countries have been changed frequently, and in 1959 a general increase of 50 per cent came into effect which was coupled with an upward adjustment of the basic quotas of Canada, West Germany and Japan, reflecting these countries' changed economic and political status since the end of the war. The 1967 Rio de Janeiro agreements have accepted these quotas as a basis for distribution of the Special Drawing Rights.

Modigliani and Kenen in their proposal urge a frequent review of these quotas, and suggest the development of a general objective formula which gives greater weight to growth in foreign trade, and fluctuations in recent years, than to the behaviour of the same variables further back in time. Roosa's plan envisages distribution of fiat reserves according to countries' average past dollar and gold holdings, though countries should have the right to accept less than the amount to which they are entitled if they so choose. This scheme would tend to lead to income transfers from less developed countries because the less developed countries have historically had small holdings of gold and dollars, and because a successful increase of liquidity in the developed nations, *ceteris paribus*, makes them more willing to run deficits with the rest of the world, and these deficits involve the net transfer of real resources to them. While the less developed countries end up with more gold or convertible currencies, the developed countries, nevertheless, under these circumstances have succeeded in increasing their command over real resources as a direct result of the fiat liquidity creation and its formula for distribution.

How Many Reserves to Create

Just as national central banks creating fiat money have to make continuous policy decisions as to the rate at which they increase the money supply, the level of credit tightness and the level of interest rates, so an agency responsible for the creation of international reserves will have to face analytically equivalent issues. But while there is much disagreement among economists whether the proper targets for domestic monetary policy should be rates of increase in money supply, interest rates or free reserves, all discussions about international reserve creation focus on the question of the rate of increase in the stock of reserves.

Theoretically, the model developed in Part One of this book implies that given institutional and structural characteristics of the world and given the levels of income and world trade, there is at any moment in time one unique supply of international reserves, which in conjunction with the proper national propensities to make income, price and other adjustment, to give up national sovereignty etc., and permits the world economy to operate at a welfare maximizing level. Consequently, between any two periods in time there is also one unique, optimum rate of growth in reserves. It has already been discussed how difficult it is to estimate this optimum rate of increase, not only because of conceptual ambiguities but also because of the difficulties of measurement.

Practical solutions to the problem of deciding how many reserves to create each time period cannot wait until these conceptual and measurement problems are resolved and are therefore based on two broad categories of simple approaches. The first starts with the basic decision of how much to create in the aggregate and then distributes the implied quantity to the individual countries in proportion to long-run average demand as under the Rio de Janeiro Agreements or some other criteria, as under the Stamp and Triffin plans. The annual rate of increase is to be agreed upon through a process of political bargaining and ultimately voting among members belonging to the world monetary organization. There are many possible institutionally different ways of arriving at a figure for each year. Triffin proposes a constant rate which can be changed by annual voting of a qualified majority. However, he leaves details to negotiations. The Rio de Janeiro proposals envisage setting up targets by voting of an 85 per cent majority. These targets would determine annual rates of increase in reserves for the following 5 years. It is clear that the actual choice of how the targets are derived in itself involves political bargaining with each country identifying a certain procedure as being in its own interest.

The second method starts with the determination of individual countries' demand and through aggregation arrives at the quantity of total reserves to be created. However, the basic principle of individual demand determination is modified by Roosa in that he would permit countries only a maximum rate of annual increase, though they may opt for less than this maximum. Modigliani and Kenen propose the development of an index measuring each country's long-run demand for reserves, which according to the analysis in the last part of chapter 3 is determined by such objective criteria as the level of foreign trade, and standard deviation of fluctuations in this trade, and which therefore are to be used to compute the index. Each country's demand is recomputed annually and the quantity to be distributed depends on the difference between the computed demand and the total quantity a country had actually received in the past. The sum of reserves to which individual countries are entitled determines the aggregate quantity to be created.

The problem of choosing a proper rate of international reserve creation can be solved in many different ways, each of which has its own advantages and disadvantages. Economists and those who distrust the wisdom of politicians voting for reserve increases favour objective measures requiring no political judgements, such as the one used in the system proposed by Modigliani and Kenen and by constant rates of increase subject to infrequent changes as proposed by Triffin. Others, who distrust technicians and dislike leaving man's destiny with fixed rules, prefer the time-consuming, often frustrating process of political bargaining, which tends to give results sensitive to majority tastes and changing technical characteristics of world trade and finance. There is little doubt that the Western world is moving towards the latter type of solution, as is evidenced by the Rio de Janeiro Agreements.

The Place of Gold

The historic evolution of national monetary systems has shown that convertibility of paper money into some ultimate standard of value or commodity with an intrinsic value of its own, such as gold, is neither a necessary nor a sufficient condition for the successful working of these systems. In fact, while the first national central banks in the Western world permitted their citizens to exchange bank notes into gold or silver at any time, banking and monetary crises did occur and may have been aggravated by the speculative flights from paper money into gold possible under the system. On the other hand, since the thirties and after the Second World War the monetary systems have been relatively free of crises even though (or perhaps because?) nearly all national central banks have made their notes inconvertible.

These lessons, flowing from the experience of national monetary authorities, apparently failed to impress the architects of world monetary reform because most of them envisage the retention of gold as the ultimate standard of value. However, nearly all plans by scholarly authors such as those by Keynes, Triffin and Modigliani–Kenen express the hope that gold ultimately may be removed from its central position in the world monetary order. They state more or less explicitly that the retention of gold's position in their plans is designed only to make their proposals initially more acceptable to certain conservative elements and powerful special interests in the world of finance.

All proposals for reform choose *to define* the unit value of the fiat money in terms of gold, which for convenience is always the gold content of one U.S. dollar. In a sense this method of defining value is merely an efficient accounting device because, since all national currencies' par values under the I.M.F. rules are expressed either in terms of gold content or as a fraction of the dollar, the exchange value of all currencies against the fiat unit is automatically determined. However, this exchange value can be set also independently of any reference to gold or the dollar by the simple expedient of each country defining the value of its exchange rate with the fiat unit as a numeraire. The retention of gold as the numeraire by all recent reform proposals has the important and unfortunate psychological effect of retaining the metal's historic central position as ultimate standard of value.

More important than gold's role as unit of account is

the extent to which it remains convertible into national currencies. Under the Keynes plan, gold was designed to keep circulating among national central banks along with the new fiat money, but the convertibility of the fiat money at the central authority was only in one direction: countries could obtain fiat money for gold but had no right to demand gold for the fiat money. According to Keynes, the central authority's gold acquisitions from this kind of exchange were to be distributed periodically among the holders of the fiat money. Under the Modigliani–Kenen plan the central authority similarly would buy but never sell gold for fiat money.

The Bretton Woods Agreements for the I.M.F. provide that initially each country paid to the Fund in gold the smaller of either 25 per cent of its quota or 10 per cent of its official gold and U.S. dollar reserves at the time it joined the I.M.F. Countries which have 'borrowed' convertible currencies from the I.M.F. through sale of their own currencies to the institution are required to liquidate the loan by repurchasing their own currencies with gold whenever the Fund's holdings of these currencies exceeded the country's quota over a certain, specified length of time. There are no provisions in the Agreements requiring the Fund ever to pay out gold it acquired through initial subscriptions or the repurchase of national currencies. As a result of this one-way convertibility, the price of gold would have a lower but no upper limit if the United States did not supply one at $35 an ounce. Since 1956 the Fund has bought over $1 million U.S. Treasury Bills with gold, allegedly for the purpose of obtaining an interest income for its operation. However, the sterility of gold in the Fund's possession and the declining U.S. gold stock in the face of the dollar's key role in the system have given added significance to, and quite possibly provide the real rationale for, these gold transfers.

Under the Triffin plan, countries would be obliged to hold a certain and fixed percentage of their total international reserve assets in the form of deposits with the central agency. These deposits can be acquired initially only through the surrender of gold or currencies convertible into gold. Countries would agree to accept such deposits in settlement of their international claims without limit, but would have the right to convert into gold all of those deposits accrued to them in excess of this minimum requirement. This right to convertibility is a potentially serious source of instability as the central agency increases members' deposits through open market operations and lending. Triffin suggests a series of measures allegedly having the effect of reducing the danger of a liquidity crisis for the central authority, such as increasing deposit requirements or the declaration of a 'gold scarcity'. However, these measures are unsatisfactory because they fail to eliminate gold's basic role as the ultimate standard of value and it is clear that the convertibility provision of the Triffin plan is one of its most serious weaknesses.

Under the Rio de Janeiro Agreements setting up the Special Drawing Rights, the reformed I.M.F. itself does not hold any gold. However, the metal retains a central role in the system. Under the Agreements each country receives a certain quantity of S.D.R.s as determined by the over-all increase in the stock of those assets and the country's share according to its quota. These S.D.R.s can be used by owners to acquire dollars or any other currencies needed to intervene in the foreign exchange markets, and each country is obligated to accept these S.D.R.s in quantities up to two times its cumulative past allocations of S.D.R. The problem of gold convertibility enters into this mechanism if countries use their S.D.R.s to acquire, say, dollars or francs, and then exchange these currencies for gold at the U.S. or French central banks. To guard against such a possibility, the Agreements provide that S.D.R.s can be used only to meet speculative attack and never to change a country's reserve composition.

The nature of the scholarly proposals and the Rio de Janeiro Agreements suggests that gold is destined to retain its position as standard of value under systems of centrally created reserves, much as it has under the gold exchange standard. However, the history of national monetary standards raises the hope that gold may be removed eventually from this position, as the world becomes accustomed to holding and making payments with the fiat money, as a matter of routine. Once this stage has been reached there exists an effective substitute for gold and it may then become feasible to rid the world of the cross of gold by making all national currencies and the fiat money inconvertible. Gold will then be priced so that production suffices to meet the demand for industrial and ornamental purposes.

At the 17 March 1968 meeting of central bankers in Washington agreement was reached on the establishment of a two-price system for gold, according to which central banks will continue to transfer gold among themselves at $35 an ounce, while its price in the free market will be left to find its own level. One of the problems with this system is that if the free market price is above $35, any central bank can reap substantial profits by arbitraging the two prices. As a result of such arbitrage the gold stock available for intergovernmental settlements is diminished, and ultimately could become zero.

In order to protect the system against this possibility central banks pledged to refrain from such arbitrage, and it was agreed that national monetary authorities would refuse to buy any gold in the open market so that the entire current production of the metal would be available to satisfy the free market demand. It was hoped that this current production would keep the free market price near, or even below the price of $35, at which the central banks were transferring gold among each other, thus reducing profitability of arbitraging by central banks.

Reports circulated that if in spite of these precautions and agreements official monetary gold were to leak into the free market, it would be necessary to protect the system further by prohibiting the removal of all physical stocks of gold from the vaults of the United States. Transfer of 'ownership' of the gold among central banks would be undertaken by moving it from sellers' to buyers' cages within the vault.[2]

It remains to be seen whether such a treatment of the physical gold stock will be adopted officially, and if so whether it will operate successfully. However, the fact that the world central banks have separated a pool of gold for special treatment in the manner described, and that there was the discussion of physical imprisonment is symptomatic of the evolutionary demonetization of gold. The agreement not to increase or decrease the stock of monetary gold implies that an ever decreasing proportion of the world's official reserves will be backed by the metal. The next logical step following the physical imprisonment is that transfers among banks will take place through mere book-keeping entries, rather than the physical transfer between cages in the vault. After the system has operated successfully for some time in this fashion it will become obvious that the buried stock of gold is of no consequence for the system's effectiveness, and the metal can be sold in the free market for industrial and ornamental uses. At this time gold will be demonetized completely.

Maintenance of the Fiat Money Value

Under the gold standard no provision has to be made to assure the real purchasing power of gold. In a two-country world, if all prices double, the value of gold in current prices also doubles and its holders are assured constant real exchange value in the commodity markets of both countries A and B. Theoretically, if prices in A double but remain constant in B, A's exchange rate falls by half and consequently gold holdings in country B maintain their value in exchange for A's real goods; gold held in country A doubles in price along with the prices of all other commodities so that its value remains undiminished.

2. During the operation of the gold exchange standard the vaults of the Federal Reserve Bank of New York contained wire cages, rented by foreign central banks, into which gold was transferred and stored.

Such a maintenance of money's purchasing power is not assured automatically under the fiat money standard. In a two-country world, a general doubling of prices fails to result in any balance-of-payments difficulties, changes in the relative value of the currencies or the rate at which they are exchanged into the fiat money unit. Yet, the country which is a net creditor to the other as a result of having run a balance-of-payments surplus, and having transferred real resources finds that the fiat money it had received in payment for these resources, brings only one half as many after the world price level had doubled. This phenomenon is well known from monetary theory as the inflation tax on holders of money. Just as national governments have failed to arrange for compensation of inflation losses to money holders, so all of the plans for world monetary reform have omitted provisions for the compensation of creditors and for taxation of debtors in the international payments system.

However, all reform plans provide a value guarantee for international fiat money of the following kind. In a two-country world if country A's prices double but country B's don't, then country A faces balance-of-payments deficits and ultimately has to halve the value of its currency. Under a world monetary system where creditor country B holds A's national obligations denominated in A's currency units, such a devaluation cuts in half the resource value of B's reserve holdings. This phenomenon is the well known exchange risk attached to foreign exchange holdings. The scholarly reform plans and the Rio de Janeiro Agreements eliminate this risk by providing for an exchange or gold guarantee for the fiat unit. In practice this guarantee is achieved by fixing the national currency units' exchange value in terms of the fiat money either directly or through gold. As a result, a devaluation automatically increases the fiat money's exchange value in terms of the devalued currency by exactly the proportion of the devaluation. For example, when country A devalues in terms of the fiat money unit, B's holdings of fiat money can be exchanged for a number of A's currency units increased exactly proportionately to the devaluation and the inflation in A.

These exchange guarantees make the fiat money superior to national currencies as reserve assets. However, the absence of protection against general and world-wide inflation makes the fiat money inferior to gold under the gold standard. But fiat money with an exchange guarantee is no better and no worse than gold under the gold exchange standard where the price of gold is fixed and unresponsive to general price level changes. World-wide economic efficiency would be increased theoretically if a world monetary authority would tax net debtors and compensate net creditors to avoid inter-country redistributions of wealth due to inflation. Such a tax would be easy to administer and theoretically should be based on price changes revealed by a world-wide index. This point will be discussed in some more detail at the end of this chapter.

In the context of the present discussion, it is important to note that exchange guarantees attached to fiat money do not assure the preservation of purchasing power of foreign assets unless all countries meet balance-of-payments disequilibria through devaluation. For example, if a country has gone through a domestic inflation and remedies its resultant balance-of-payments deficits not through devaluation but through the imposition of import duties and direct controls on trade, then this nation's creditors holding fiat money can obtain resources only at the old exchange rate and at inflated prices. An effective functioning of the exchange guarantee mechanism therefore requires that countries abstain from the use of tariffs, exchange controls and other direct methods, to influence their international payments positions.

Adjustment to Payments Imbalances

The analysis of chapters 5 and 6 has shown that under the system of flexible exchange rates, and under the gold standard, adjustment of international trade to imbalances occurs automatically through changes in exchange rates, or domestic prices and incomes, in both the deficit and surplus countries. On the other hand, under the gold exchange standard, and a system of fixed exchange rates with fiat reserves, there exists no such *automatic* adjustment mechanism affecting both the deficit and surplus countries. Deficit countries face the unavoidable reality that their international reserve assets and credits are finite, but surplus countries can accumulate international reserves indefinitely, subject only to their ability to sterilize the inflow of foreign currency and to prevent it from having an inflationary effect on the domestic money supply. As a result, the burden of adjustment tends to fall almost exclusively on the deficit countries, even though worldwide efficiency most often tends to be served by a more equal sharing of the adjustment burden by both surplus and deficit countries, as under the gold standard or flexible exchange rates.

As had been argued in the theoretical analysis of Part One of this book, the creation of fiat money is designed to endow all countries with sufficient reserves so that they can minimize the adjustment burden associated with deficits through the use of slower working, but less costly, adjustment policies. This kind of slower adjustment is highly desirable in the case of unavoidable disturbances to international payments equilibrium, such as changes in taste or technology, natural catastrophes or honest errors in policy making. However, these larger reserves also lend themselves to abuse in that they can be used to pay for balance-of-payments deficits caused by domestic inflationary policies, which practically force the rest of the world to lend to the deficit countries and which tend to have an inflationary impact on the economies of the surplus countries.

The absence of an automatic adjustment mechanism working on surplus countries under a system of centrally created reserves therefore has the two undesirable consequences of, first, putting the adjustment burden on deficit countries and, second, providing more means by which countries can pursue domestic inflationary policies and force the rest of the world to lend to them. Most plans for international monetary reform, based on a central money creating authority, have made provisions to eliminate or at least reduce the severity of these consequences.

Theoretically such provisions can be based on two widely different principles. First, countries can be asked to *co-operate voluntarily* and act in the interest of world welfare maximization. Such co-operation is to be based on a universally accepted code of behaviour, such as the one known as 'following the rules of the game', which assumes the automatic and equitable working of the adjustment mechanism. Under the weak version of this code countries do not interfere with the domestic consequences which balance-of-payments surpluses or deficits have on the money supply and income. Under the strong version countries voluntarily adopt monetary policies which have the same consequences as gold flows would have had under the gold standard, thus reinforcing the changes in the money supply and income incurred by the balance-of-payments surplus or deficit. Such voluntary co-operation has not been successful, primarily because it frequently runs against the national interest of certain countries and in its basic design has the same undesirable effects as the gold standard proper, which was discussed in chapter 6 above. However, in principle at least the code's weak version might increase the overall functioning of a world monetary system based on fiat money creation. Adoption of a pledge spelling out a general set of behavioural principles along these lines, together with the agreement for the setting up of a central reserve-creating agency, could do little harm but might have important benefits.

The second basic approach to the problem of adjustment employs *economic pressure* on countries to share the adjustment burden and to protect creditor nations from inflationary influences. The logical agent for the enforcement of this pressure is the fiat money-issuing agency itself, and some plans for a monetary order based on fiat money envision its use in this fashion. However, these plans differ with respect to the timing, intensity and nature of these pressures.

Theoretically, the optimum use of these pressures encourages countries to use just the proper domestic income and price adjustments, devaluation, direct controls and financing of deficits with fiat money as is demanded by a world welfare maximizing monetary system. The theoretical discussions of Part One have shown how difficult it is in practice to determine when each country acts in this theoretically optimum fashion, and the same difficulties are encountered in getting the central agency to apply the proper pressures at the proper time. Because of these difficulties essentially mechanical rules for the application of pressures and protection of creditors have been developed. All of these rules have in common that they make the timing and intensity of the pressures a function of the cumulative size and duration of countries' deficits, relative to the total size of the fiat money initially distributed to them. Furthermore, they set a limit on the quantity of fiat money any country is required to accept. The pressures themselves take the form of, first, insisting that governments adopt certain domestic policies before any further credit money is issued to them and second, the imposition of interest rate charges.

Under the original Keynes plan countries with debit *or* credit balances with the agency would pay interest on a graduated scale: zero if the balances are one quarter of their quota, one per cent if they are between one quarter and one half and two per cent if they are above one half. These interest charges, quite low in light of post-World War Two levels of interest rates, but quite high in view of pre-war levels, were considered to be an incentive for both creditor and debtor countries to aim for balance in their international payments.

However, the Keynes plan did not rely entirely on the

interest rate charges to encourage adjustment. It envisaged that countries cannot increase their debit balance by more than a quarter of their quota within one year without permission from the agency's governing board. Furthermore, countries with debit balances exceeding one half of their quota may be required by the board to deposit collateral of gold or domestic bonds, devalue, or impose other policies to improve the balance of payments. Similar, increasingly more severe restrictions on the freedom of member countries were envisaged if debit balances became larger proportions of quotas. The ultimate pressure was that a country could be declared as being in default with the agency and lose the right to further fiat money drawings. The Keynes plan had as one of its distinguishing features the application of similar pressures on *credit* countries.

The International Monetary Fund's lending policy is to provide member countries with *temporary* assistance during their efforts to find solutions for balance of payments. However, the quantity of loans made in total and per time period are governed by increasingly greater restrictions the greater a country's outstanding obligations to the Fund.

The mechanics of obtaining loans from the Fund involve the borrowing country's 'purchase' (or 'drawing') of other member countries' currencies from the Fund in return for the borrowing country's own currency. Any country can obtain foreign currencies with the greatest of ease up to a sum equal to 25 per cent of its quota. At such a level of borrowing the Fund holds that country's currency valued at 100 per cent of its quota because, as was discussed above, one requirement of I.M.F. membership is that a sum of domestic currency equal to 75 per cent of any country's quota be deposited with the Fund.

Additional drawings from the Fund are limited to sums up to 25 per cent of the quota during any 12-month period. In total the Fund's holdings of any country's currency must not exceed 200 per cent of its quota.

Repayment of loans from the Fund are effected by the borrower's repurchase of his own currency or through another member's purchase of that currency. As a general rule repayment must take place within a period not exceeding 3 to 5 years. Moreover, countries which have accumulated a stock of international reserves exceeding their quotas must repurchase their currencies at an accelerated pace.

Fundamentally, these repayment requirements are responsible for the fact that the I.M.F. created at Bretton Woods has not been able to increase the world supply of genuinely owned reserves. Repayment of a loan from the Fund extinguishes the purchasing power the initial exchange transaction had created. Because of this feature, and because countries had to surrender gold at the Fund's creation, it can be said that the Fund has actually reduced owned world reserves by the amount of the initial gold deposits. Any plans for expansion of the Fund's role in international finance had to face this important fact squarely. Thus, a simple increase in the Fund's quotas did not serve to increase aggregate reserves in the way envisaged by Keynes, Triffin and under the Rio de Janeiro Agreements, though such increases served to raise aggregate *borrowing* facilities of nations.

The International Monetary Fund provides for the imposition of interest rate charges to countries whenever the Fund's holdings of their currencies exceeds the size of their quota. Rates on excess holdings increase with the size and the duration of these debit balances. When the charges have reached 4 per cent the country is obligated to consult with the I.M.F. on measures to reduce the balances. However, in practice, the role of interest charges as a means of attaining adjustment has been overshadowed by the method of attaching conditions to the granting of credits in the manner just discussed.

Under the Bretton Woods Agreements creditor countries can be subjected to pressures only through invocation of the 'scarce currency clause'. Basically this clause was designed to guard against the possibility that member countries' aggregate demand for a specific currency arising from their gold and first tranche credit lines would exceed the Fund's holding of that currency. Such a declaration authorizes member countries to use discriminatory exchange restrictions in their dealings with that specific currency. In the history of the Fund this clause has never been invoked.

Under the Rio de Janeiro Agreements no provisions were made to encourage adjustment by surplus countries. To the contrary, surplus countries are protected in the sense that none are required to accept the fiat money in quantities greater than twice their past allotments. Thus a country with cumulative past allotments of $500 million is required to accept a maximum of $1000 million of *additional* fiat money in settlement of payments surpluses with the rest of the world. Moreover, the fiat money balances are planned to pay a modest rate of interest.

There is a similar lack of any real pressures on debtor countries, except for the provision that an average balance of 30 per cent of past fiat money allotments must be maintained over any 5-year period. This provision in principle is the same as the requirement for the maintenance of a minimum deposit often associated with commercial bank loans. It has the simple real effect of lowering the size of the loan and in the case of the reformed I.M.F. of reducing the effective quantity below the nominal sum of fiat money created. Debtors have to make no explicit interest payments. However, they do forego the interest accruing to the holders of the fiat money balances.

Under the Triffin plan similarly there are no official pressures to make adjustments on debtor or creditor nations except for the interest payments to creditors and the implicit opportunity cost of the funds debtors have to pay to creditors.

If one considers the institution of a fiat-money-creating agency in the broad context of a smoothly functioning international economy, the absence of any real economic pressures on surplus countries under the Rio de Janeiro Agreements represents a serious deficiency. As a result, there exists the possibility that the new world monetary order, based on the creation of fiat money, will have a deflationary tendency in spite of massive creations of liquidity. Such a deflation might occur if governments continue to act nationalistically, and one or more of the major industrial countries of the world operate their economies at low levels of capacity, keeping prices relatively more stable than the rest of the world and incurring large balance-of-payments surpluses. As soon as these countries have reached the limit of their required holdings of fiat money the rest of the world is obliged to meet further deficits with gold, whose supply is not expected to increase. As a result, the deficit countries will be forced to devalue, which may be harmful to world trade and welfare and which is likely to be accompanied by disturbing foreign exchange speculation, or to impose inefficient direct restrictions on trade and capital movements, or to slow down the level of domestic economic activity.

Perhaps such a bias has been built into the Rio de Janeiro Agreements on purpose in order to increase the probability that the world price level remains relatively stable. Such price stability is favoured by many conservative elements in Western capitalist societies for a variety of reasons. Whatever the merit of these reasons in the long run perspective of human civilization and economic development, the particular method chosen for enforcement is essentially undemocratic in that it gives undue power to a small group of countries, whichever they may be in the future, to force the rest of the world into having greater price stability than it desires or into the acceptance of welfare-reducing adjustment policies. Perhaps democratic processes are unsuitable for major decision making in economic matters, such as the world-wide rate of price increases, so that 'democracy must be protected from itself' by built-in institutional constraints. There are no clear-cut answers to these issues.

The Rio de Janeiro Agreements

While this book was in the process of being written, the signing of the Rio de Janeiro and Washington Agreements have moved the world significantly closer to the establishment of a world monetary system based on the central creation of international reserves to be called Special Drawing Rights, S.D.R. As a result, the major features of the most likely future monetary order are becoming clear and the last pages of this chapter are the fitting place for their brief review and integration into the analytical structure of the preceding discussion.

First of all it is worth pointing out that the Rio de Janeiro Agreements permit the creation of genuine fiat money. National governments can use the majority of their S.D.R. holdings as if they were owned. Foreign exchange, gold or dollar reserves and the S.D.R.s circulate without being extinguished through repayment.

The problem of seigniorage distribution has been solved by the demand type method through the use of the existing I.M.F. quotas. Countries are thus entitled to allocations of S.D.R.s according to their long-run average demand for them. As was argued above, this demand is presumably reflected in the size of their foreign trade and past reserve holdings which served as the basis on which the I.M.F. quotas under the Bretton Woods Agreements were derived. Countries have the option not to accept some of their periodic allocations of S.D.R.s if they so desire. No new mechanism has been created which would assure the periodic review of each country's quota in the system.

The quantity of reserves to be created each year is decided by an 85 per cent majority vote by the Board of Governors. It is important to note that the members of the European Common Market have a voting strength equivalent to 16 per cent so that by voting as a block these countries can veto all actions on reserve increases.

Under the Rio de Janeiro Agreements, the S.D.R. mechanism operates without any provisions for settlement in gold, except that the fiat money cannot be used to draw national currencies which are then exchanged into gold at the country's central bank. Outside of the system of S.D.R. creation and administration, gold retains its role as the ultimate standard of value. However, the Washington Agreements establishing a two-price system for gold, $35 an ounce for settlement among central banks and a free market price for private gold users, is designed to protect the system from speculative instabilities and to lead to a gradual demonetization of gold.

The maintenance of the fiat money's value is assured as a result of the fact that national currency exchange rates are defined in terms of the fiat unit. Therefore, the value of one S.D.R. expressed in terms of a national currency increases or decreases proportionately to the national currency's devaluation or appreciation, respectively. However, the value of the S.D.R.s is not protected against over-all world price increases.

The Rio de Janeiro Agreements envision no institutional changes which would make international adjustments to payments imbalances more automatic than they have been under the gold exchange standard. The main pressures for adjustment will continue to be on the deficit countries in danger of running out of reserves.

It is convenient to explain additional specific institutional characteristics of the system with the help of an example which illustrates the creation, distribution and use of S.D.R.s.

Consider the situation where the Board of Governors has decided by a 85 per cent majority vote to increase S.D.R.s by $1 billion over a period of 12 months. Country A, whose quota represents 10 per cent of all quotas in the International Monetary Fund, receives a share of new S.D.R.s worth $100 million.

When country A needs to intervene in the foreign exchange markets, in order to prevent its currency from depreciating and exchanging at a price outside of the official intervention points, it notifies the Fund of its intent to withdraw usable national currencies in exchange for its S.D.R.s.

The Fund then notifies country A which member country's or countries' reserve position it considers to be satisfactory and whose currencies can be withdrawn. Consider that country A thus attains $50 million of country B's currency. The Fund, through internal book-keeping entries reduces country A's and increases country B's S.D.R. holdings by $50 million. Furthermore, it charges a modest interest rate, foreseen to be 1·5 per cent, to the debtor nation and pays the same rate to the creditor.

Country A or any other country does not have to repay any national currencies it obtained for fiat money as long as it maintains a holding of S.D.R.s equal to 30 per cent of past allotments, where the holdings are computed as a 5-year moving average. Country B or any other country is obliged to accept S.D.R.s only up to the point where their total holdings are equal to three times the amount of S.D.R.s allocated to it by the Fund.

References

Chapter 1

For general theoretical analysis of international monetary problems see the widely used undergraduate textbook by Kindleberger (1963), the Hart and Kenen (1964) section on international finance, and the crop of new texts putting greater emphasis on the financial aspects of international economics – Mundell (1968a), Root, Kramer and D'Arlin (1966), Tew (1967) and Ward (1965). At the level for graduate students there is the new and thorough book by Yeager (1966) and the classic by Meade (1951). Theoretical essays on general international monetary problems by a group of young economists are found in Mundell (1968a). Johnson (1965) surveys some of the most important theoretical issues and (1967a) puts the international monetary problems into the broader context of international tariff and lending policies. For the flavour of policy making in the face of political realities see Gardner (1956), Harrod (1951) and Scammell (1964).

The most articulate and perceptive analysis of international monetary problems in the post-war period, made especially forceful because it identifies with a cause, is found in Triffin (1961).

Chapter 2

For a summary of the main institutional features and analytical implications of alternative forms of international monetary organization see Johnson (1962), Machlup (1962) and *International Monetary Arrangements: The*

Problem of Choice (1964). In Grubel (1963) and Hinshaw (1967) the most important plans for reform of the international monetary system have been reprinted. (See also bibliography to chapters 5–8.) Machlup (1964) presents the theory of the foreign exchange market uesful for an understanding of government intervention analysis of chapter 2.

Chapter 3

For a detailed analysis of the exchange market, price and income effects, tariffs and direct controls see Kindleberger (1963), Meade (1951), Mundell (1968) and Yeager (1966). On the benefits from international co-operation see Cooper (1967). The role of international short-term capital flows is discussed in Bloomfield (1946), Grubel (1966), Meade (1951) and Stoll (1968). An historic account of the disturbing nature of short-term capital flows during the thirties is found in Nurkse (1944). Ingram's perceptive analysis of the beneficial effects of capital movements is found in Ingram (1962). Attempts to measure the demand for reserves by individual countries have been made by Heller (1966), and Kenen and Yudin (1965).

Chapter 4

A thorough scholarly analysis of the concept and measurement of adequacy of reserves is found in Clement, Pfister and Rothwell (1967). Scholarly discussion of a theoretical optimum level of reserves with slightly different emphasis is found in Balogh (1960) and Fleming (1961 and 1967).

Readings on the basic plans for monetary reform have already been supplied in chapter 2.

Chapter 5

Hume (1752) presents the basic, classical model of the gold standard. Bloomfield (1959), Brown (1940), Ford

(1962), Mertens (1944) and Triffin (1947) are the most recent theoretical-empirical studies of the gold standard system. Heilperin (1962) and Rueff (1961) urge the re-introduction of the gold standard in place of the gold exchange standard.

Chapter 6

The case for flexible exchange rates is made best by Friedman (1953), Meade (1955) and Sohmen (1961). The views of prominent economists opposing flexible exchange rates are found in *Factors Affecting the U.S. Balance of Payments* (1962). McKinnon (1963) and Mundell (1961) take the flexible exchange rate argument into new grounds by introducing and extending the notion of optimum currency areas.

A scholarly analysis of and contribution to arguments for and against flexible exchange rates as well as a discussion of historical experiences is found in Clement, Pfister and Rothwell (1967) and Yeager (1966). Aliber (1962) and Rhomberg (1964) are case studies of periods when some countries actually had flexible rates.

The controversy over destabilizing and stabilizing speculation has been pushed forward by Baumol (1957 and 1959), Eastman (1958), Lerner (1944), Meade (1949–50 and 1955), Telser (1959) and Tsiang (1957 and 1958). Black (1966) and Murphy (1965) propose the introduction of modified flexibility.

Chapter 7

Theoretical models explaining the essentials of the gold exchange standard mechanisms have been worked out by Kenen (1960) and Triffin (1961).

The history of the gold exchange standard before the First World War is found in Nurkse (1944). The recent problems of the current system were analysed in Aliber (1966), Lary (1963) and Triffin (1961). Special attention is given to the role of the world banker in Grubel (1964, 1965) and the ensuing controversy with Aliber (1965) and Goldstein (1965).

The theoretical problem of seigniorage is presented in Grubel (1968) and Johnson (1967a).

The working of the gold exchange standard is analysed and improvements for its operation are suggested by Bernstein (1963), Jacobson (1962), Lutz (1963), Posthuma (1963), Roosa (1962), Wallich (1961) and Zolotas (1961, 1962).

Chapter 8

The Central Government Solution is presented by Stamp (1962). The problems of commodity-backed money are discussed in Friedman (1951), Graham (1944), Grubel (1965), Hart, Kaldor and Tinbergen (1964) and Johnson (1967). For the Hirschman linkage effects see Hirschman (1958).

The Transactions Demand solution has a theoretical foundation in Tobin (1956). The White Plan is explained in Gardner (1956) and Harrod (1951). The Keynes plan reference is Keynes (1943). Most useful information on the International Monetary Fund is found in Horie (1964). The Rio de Janeiro Agreements (1956) have been reprinted in 'Agreement on plan for creating special drawing rights'. References to the articles by Bernstein, Posthuma and Lutz have been made in chapter 7. For the arguments of Modigliani and Kenen see (1966) and of Roosa see (1965).

Criticism of the role of gold under the Triffin plan were made by Altman (1961) and Angell (1961).

On the problems of adjustment see Mundell (1965); the 'rules of the game' have been discussed by Bloomfield (1959) and Nurkse (1944).

Aliber, R. Z. (1962), 'Speculation in the foreign exchanges: the European experience, 1919–26', *Yale Econ. Essays*, vol. 2.

Aliber, R. Z. (1965), 'The benefits and costs of being the world banker: a comment', *Nat. Bank. Rev.*, vol. 2.

Aliber, R. Z. (1966), *The Future of the Dollar as an International Currency*, Praeger.

Altman, O. (1961), 'Professor Triffin on international liquidity and the role of the Fund', *I.M.F. Staff Papers*, vol. 8. (Reprinted in Grubel (1963).)

Angell, J. (1961), 'The reorganization of the international monetary system: an alternative proposal', *Econ. J.*, vol. 71. (Reprinted in Grubel (1963).)

Balogh, T. (1960), 'International reserves and liquidity', *Econ. J.*, vol. 70. (Reprinted in Grubel (1963).)

Baumol, W. J. (1957), 'Speculation, profitability and stability', *Rev. Econ. Stat.*, vol. 39.

Baumol, W. J. (1959), 'Reply', *Rev. Econ. Stat.*, vol. 41.

Bernstein, E. M. (1963), 'Proposed reforms in the International Monetary System', *Outlook for United States Balance of Payments*, Hearings 14 December, Joint Economic Committee, Sub-Committee on International Exchange and Payments, Washington, 1963. (Reprinted in Grubel (1963).)

Black, J. (1966). 'A proposal for the reform of exchange rates', *Econ. J.*, vol. 76.

Bloomfield, A. I. (1946), 'Post-war control of international capital movements', *Amer. Econ. Rev.*, vol., 36.

Bloomfield, A. I. (1959), *Monetary Policy under the International Gold Standard: 1800–1914*, Federal Reserve Bank of New York.

Brown, W. A., Jr (1940), *The International Gold Standard Reinterpreted 1914–34*, National Bureau of Economic Research, New York.

Clement, M. O., Pfister, R. L., and Rothwell, K. J. (1967), *Theoretical Issues in International Economics*, Houghton-Mifflin.

Cooper, R. (1968), *The Economics of Interdependence*, McGraw-Hill.

Eastman, H. C. (1958), 'Aspects of speculation in the Canadian market for foreign exchanges', *Canad. J. Econ. Polit. Sci.*, vol. 24.

Factors Affecting the U.S. Balance of Payments (1962), Subcommittee on International Exchange and Payments of the Joint Economic Committee, U.S. Congress, 87th Congress, 2nd Session.

Federal Reserve System (1962), 'A system of fluctuating exchange rates: pro and con', *State of the Economy and Policies for Full Employment*, Hearings, Joint Economic Committee, U.S. Congress, 87th Congress, 2nd Session.

Fleming, J. M. (1961), 'International liquidity: end and means', *I.M.F. Staff Papers*, vol. 8.

Fleming, J. M. (1967), 'Toward assessing the need for international reserves', *Essays in International Finance*, no. 58, Princeton University Press.

Ford, A. G. (1962), *The Gold Standard 1880–1914, Britain and Argentina*, Clarendon Press.

Friedman, M. (1951), 'Commodity reserve currency', *J. Polit. Econ.*, vol. 59.

Friedman, M. (1953), 'The case for flexible exchange rates', *Essays in Positive Economics*, University of Chicago Press.

Friedman, M. (1968), 'The role of monetary policy', *Amer. Econ. Rev.*, vol. 58.

Gardner, R. N. (1956), *Sterling-Dollar Diplomacy*, Oxford University Press.

Goldstein, H. N. (1965), 'Does it necessarily cost anything to be world banker?', *Nat. Bank. Rev.*, vol. 2.

Graham, B. (1944), *World Commodities and World Currency*, McGraw-Hill.

Grubel, H.G. (1963), *International Monetary Reform: Plans and Issues*, Stanford University Press and Oxford University Press.

Grubel, H. G. (1964, 1965), 'The benefits and cost of

being the World Banker', *Nat. Bank. Rev.*, vol 2.

Grubel, H. G. (1965), 'The case against an international commodity reserve currency', *Oxford Econ. Papers*, vol. 17.

Grubel, H. G. (1966), *Forward Exchange, Speculation and the International Flow of Capital*, Stanford University Press.

Grubel, H. G. (1968), 'The distribution of seigniorage from the international liquidity creation', in R. Murdell (ed.), *World Monetary Reform*, University of Chicago Press.

Harrod, R. F. (1951), *The Life of John Maynard Keynes*, Macmillan.

Harrod, R. F. (1967), 'Assessing the trade returns', *Econ. J.*, vol. 77.

Hart, A. G., Kaldor, N., and Tinbergen, J. (1964), *The Case for an International Reserve Currency*, U. N. Conference on Trade and Development, background document, E/conf. 46/P/7, Geneva.

Hart, G., and Kenen, P. (1964), *Money Debt and Economic Activity*, Prentice-Hall.

Heilperin, M. A. (1962), 'The case for going back to gold', *Fortune*.

Heller, H. (1966), 'Optimal international reserves,' *Econ. J.*, vol. 76.

Hinshaw, R. H. (1967), *Monetary Reform and the Price of Gold*, Johns Hopkins Press.

Hirschmann, A. O. (1958), *The Strategy of Economic Development*, Yale University Press.

Horie, S. (1964), *The International Monetary Fund*, St Martin's Press.

Hume, D. (1752), 'Of money', *Political Discourses*.

Ingram, J. (1962), 'A proposal for financial integration in the Atlantic Community', *Factors Affecting the United States Balance of Payments*. Compilation of studies prepared for the sub-committee on International Exchange and Payments of the Joint Economic Committee, U.S. Congress, Washington D.C.

International Monetary Arrangements: The Problem of Choice (1964), Report on the Deliberations of an International Study Group of 32 Economists, Princeton University Press.

Jacobson, P. (1962), 'The two functions of an international monetary standard: stability and liquidity', *Bulletin d'Information et de Documentation*, National Bank of Belgium, April. (Reprinted in Grubel (1963).)

Johnson H. G. (1962), 'International liquidity – problems and plans', *Malay. Econ. Rev.*, vol. 7. (Reprinted in Grubel (1963).)

Johnson, H. G. (1965), *The World Economy at the Crossroads*, Oxford University Press.

Johnson H. G. (1967a), 'Theoretical problems of the international monetary system', *Pakistan Devel. Rev.*, vol. 7.

Johnson H. G. (1967b), *Economic Policies Towards the Less Developed Countries*, The Brookings Institution.

Kenen, P. B., and Yudin, E. (1965), 'The demand for international reserves', *Rev. Econ. Stat.*, vol. 47.

Kenen, P. B. (1960), 'International liquidity and the balance of payments of a reserve currency country', *Quart. J. Econ.*, vol. 74.

Keynes, J. M. (1943), *Proposals for an International Clearing Union*, cmnd. 6434, H.M.S.O. (Reprinted in Grubel (1963).)

Kindleberger, C. P. (1963), *International Economics*, 3rd edn, Irwin.

Lary, H. (1963), *Problems of the United States as World Trader and Banker*, National Bureau of Economic Research.

Lerner, A. P. (1944), *The Economics of Control*, Macmillan.

Lutz, F. (1963), 'The problems of international liquidity and the multiple currency standard', *Essays in International Finance*, no. 41, Princeton University Press. (Reprinted in Grubel (1963).)

Machlup, F. (1943), *International Trade and the National Income Multiplier*, Blakiston.

Machlup, F. (1962), *Plans for Reforms of the International Monetary System*, Special Papers in International Economics, no. 3, Princeton University Press.

Machlup, F. (1964), 'The theory of foreign exchanges', in *International Payments, Debts and Gold. Collected Essays by F. Machlup*, Scribner.

McKinnon, R. (1963), 'Optimum currency areas', *Amer. Econ. Rev.*, vol. 53.

Meade, J. E. (1949–50), 'Degree of competitive speculation', *Rev. Econ. Stud.*, vol. 17.

Meade, J. E. (1951), *The Balance of Payments*, Oxford University Press.

Meade, J. E. (1955), 'The case for variable exchange rates', *Three Banks Rev.*, vol. 27.

Meade, J. E. (1961), 'The future of international payments', *Three Banks Rev.*, vol. 50. (Reprinted in Grubel (1963).)

Mertens, J. E. (1944), *La Naissance et le Développement de L'Etalou-Or*, Presses Universitaires de France.

Modigliani, E., and Kenen, P. (1966) 'Suggestion for solving the international liquidity problem', *Banca Nazionale del Lavoro Quart. Rev.*, vol. 76.

Mundell, R. A. (1961), 'A theory of optimum currency areas', *Amer. Econ. Rev.*, vol. 51.

Mundell, R. A. (1965), 'The proper division of the burden of international adjustment', *Nat. Bank. Rev.*, vol. 3.

Mundell, R. A. (1968a), *International Economics*, Macmillan.

Mundell, R. A. (1968b), *World Monetary Reform*, University of Chicago Press.

Murphy, C. (1965), 'Moderated exchange rate variability', *Nat. Bank. Rev.*, vol. 3.

Nurske, R. (1944), *International Currency Experience*, League of Nations, Geneva.

Phelps, E. S. (1967), 'Phillips curves, expectations of inflation and optimal unemployment over time', *Economica*, vol. 34.

Posthuma, S. (1963), 'The international monetary system', *Banca Nazionale del Lavoro Quart. Rev.*, vol. 16.

Rhomberg. R. (1964), 'A model of the Canadian economy under fixed and fluctuating exchange rates', *J. Polit. Econ.*, vol. 72.

Rio de Janeiro Agreements (1967), 'Agreement on plan for creating special drawing rights', *Fed. Res. Bull.*, vol. 53.

Roosa, R. (1962), 'Assuring the free world's liquidity', *Business Review Supplement*, Federal Reserve Bank of Philadelphia, September.

Roosa, R. V. (1965), *Monetary Reform for the World Economy*, published for the Council on Foreign Relations by Harper and Row.

Root, F., Kramer, R., and D'Arlin, M. (1966), *International Trade and Finance*, South Western Publishing Co.

Rueff, J. (1961), 'Gold exchange standard a danger to the West', *The Times*, 27–29 June. (Reprinted in Grubel (1963).)

Scammell, W. M. (1964), *International Monetary Policy*, Macmillan.

Snider, D. A. (1966), *International Monetary Relations*, Random House.

Sohmen, E. (1961), *Flexible Exchange Rates, Theory and Controversy*, University of Chicago Press.

Stamp, J. (1962), 'The Stamp Plan – 1962 version', *Moorgate and Wall Street*, Autumn. (Reprinted in Grubel, (1963).)

Stoll, H. (1968), 'An empirical study of the forward exchange market under fixed and flexible exchange rate systems', *Canad. J. Econ.*, vol. 1.

Telser, L. G. (1959), 'A theory of speculation relating profitability and stability', *Rev. Econ. Stat.*, vol. 41.

Tew, B. (1967), *International Monetary Co-operation, 1945–67*, Hutchinson University Library.

Tobin, J. (1956), 'The interest elasticity of the demand for cash', *Rev. Econ. Stat.*, vol. 38.

Triffin, R. (1947), 'National central banking and the

international economy', *International Monetary Policies*, Postwar Economic Studies, no. 7, Board of Governors of the Federal Reserve System.

Triffin, R. (1957), *Europe and the Money Muddle*, Yale University Press.

Triffin, R. (1961), *Gold and the Dollar Crisis*, Yale University Press. (Reprinted in condensed form in Grubel (1963).)

Triffin, R. (1966), *The World Money Maze*, Yale University Press.

Triffin, R. (1968), *Our International Monetary System*, Random House.

Tsiang, S. C. (1957), 'An experiment with a flexible exchange rate system: the case of Peru, 1950–54', *I.M.F. Staff Papers*, vol. 5.

Tsiang, S. C. (1958), 'A theory of foreign-exchange speculation under a floating exchange system', *J. Polit. Econ.*, vol. 66.

Tsiang, S. C. (1959), 'Fluctuating exchange rates in countries with relatively stable economies: some European experiences after World War I', *I.M.F. Staff Papers*, vol. 7.

Wallich, H. (1961), 'Co-operation to solve the gold problem', *Harv. Bus. Rev.*, vol. 39. (Reprinted in Grubel (1963).)

Ward, R. (1965), *International Finance*, Prentice-Hall.

Yeager, L. B. (1966), *International Monetary Relations*, Harper and Row.

Zolotas, X. (1961, 1962), 'Toward a reinforced gold exchange standard', *Bank of Greece Papers and Lectures*, nos. 7 and 12. (Reprinted in Grubel (1963).)

Index

Adjustment mechanism
  of debit and credit countries
    178, 179
  and developing countries
    52
  and economic pressures
    through rules 178–80
  flexible exchange rates,
    under foreign exchange
    market, influence on 36,
    37, 41
  gold exchange standard,
    under 146–7
  gold standard, under 91–4,
    176
  gold tranche 181
  and income changes 47
  and interest charges 178,
    179
  and price changes 46
  and quotas 179
  under Rio de Janeiro
    Agreements 181, 184
  and rules of the game 177
  and scarce currency clause
    180, 181
  and supra-national bank
    175–83
  under Triffin Plan 181
Africa 22, 123
Alaskan gold fields 103
Aliber, R. 189, 190
Altman, O. 190
Anchor argument
  and flexible exchange rates
    118, 119

Angell, J. 190
d'Arlin, M. 187
Asia 22, 123
Austria-Hungary 102, 103
Australia 102, 123

Balance-of-payments
  adjustments
  and co-operation 53
  and direct controls 50–52
  and tariffs 50–52
  see also Adjustment
    mechanism
Balogh, T. 188
Bank of England 92, 151
Bank for international
  settlements 55
Baumol, W. 117, 189
Belgium 55, 92
Benelux Union 55
Bernstein, E. 83, 84, 147,
  164, 190
Black, J. 126n, 189
Bloomfield, A. 15, 99, 188,
  190
Bretton Woods Agreements
  51, 55, 125, 135, 170, 180,
  183
  see also International
    Monetary Fund
Britain
  see United Kingdom
Brown, A. J. 188

California gold fields 102,
  103

Canada   23, 55, 112, 117,
  118, 165
Capital balance instability
  and demand for reserves
  72
Capital flows
  and flexible exchange rates
  113
Capital markets
  and international monetary
  reform   83
Clement, M. O.   188, 189
Central bankers
  and international monetary
  reform   76
Centrally created reserves
  see supra-national bank
Cooper, R.   188
Commodity money   29–31,
  158
Co-operation
  see International
  co-operation
Currency obligation potential
  128–31, 140

Denmark   131
Development aid
  see Foreign aid
Developing countries
  and adjustment policies
  52
  and interest payments   166
  and social seigniorage   157
Direct controls
  and balance of payments
  50–52
Discount rates
  and gold standard   100
Dollars
  and conversions into gold
  65, 133

gold content   169
and optimum currency
  areas   123
as reserves   21, 30, 164
role in gold exchange
  standard   134–7
and S.D.R.s   171
U.S. foreign liabilities   138
  see also United States

Eastman, H.   189
Economists
  and flexible exchange rates
  125
  role in society   124, 125
Effective tariff protection   25
Elasticities of price
  and economic measurement
  115
  function of time   115, 116
  pessimism and flexible
  exchange rates   114, 115
Employment stability
  and optimum currency
  areas   122
England
  see United Kingdom
European Common Market
  see European Economic
  Community
European Economic
  Community   22, 55,
  123, 184
European Free Trade Area
  55, 123
Exchange guarantees   175
Exchange rate
  market determination of
  34–44
  and official intervention   37,
  38, 41, 42
  and speculation *see*

Speculation 125

Exchange rate flexibility
and demand for reserves 31–44
and supply of reserves 33–4

Exchange rate pegging 37, 38, 41, 42

Factor mobility
and optimum currency areas 122

Federal Reserve System, U.S. 151

Fiat money 29, 31

Fiscal policy 59, 61

Fleming, M. 188

Flexible exchange rates
anchor argument 118, 119
and capital flows 113, 114
cost for trade 111, 112
cost of transition to 110, 111
and destabilizing speculation 116–18
and economists' recommendations 125
and efficiency 107–10
and elasticity pessimism 114, 115
and foreign investment composition 113
and forward exchange market 112
and inflation 117, 119
and internationalism 119, 120
and modified flexibility 109, 110
and optimum currency areas 118, 121–4
and politics 118–20, 124, 125

as prices 108
survey of proposals, for 81, 82
and welfare 43, 44

Floating exchange rates
see Flexible exchange rates

Fluctuating exchange rates
see Flexible exchange rates

Ford, J. A. 188

Foreign aid 25, 158

Foreign trade instability
and demand for reserves 72

Forward exchange 39n, 59, 61, 62, 112

Fort Knox 145

France
balance of payments of 23
on gold exchange standard 132, 133
on gold standard 102
and Group of Ten 55
as World Banker 22

Freedom
and gold standard 105

Friedman, M. 47n, 81, 189, 190

Gardner, R. N. 165, 187, 190

Genoa Conference of 1922 132

Germany
balance of payments of 23, 146
on gold standard 102
and Group of Ten 55

General Agreement on Tariffs and Trade (GATT) 51

General Agreement to borrow 149

Gold coins 102, 109

Gold
  as commodity money   29
  under gold exchange
    standard   129–31, 133,
    145
  and I.M.F.   170
  as monetary reserves   37,
    42, 136
  and national money supplies
    49, 169
  physical imprisonment of
    173
  and Rio de Janeiro
    Agreements   184
  as standard of value   101,
    102, 169
  and supra-national bank
    168–73
  under two-price system
    172
  value, history of   64, 99
  under Washington
    Agreements   172
Gold bullion standard   98
Gold exchange standard
  and adjustment mechanism
    146–7
  and bankers: liquidity
    position   130, 138–40,
  and seigniorage distribution
    144–5
  and co-operation   147
  crisis of 1960   137, 140
  currency obligation potential
    128–31, 140
  dilemma of   137, 141
  failure of   133, 134
  formal agreement needed
    134
  and Genoa Conference
    132, 133
  and gold   145, 146

  gold economizing   129–30
  and gold guarantees   147,
    149
  during gold standard   131,
    132
  history of   78, 131–47
  and I.M.F.   135, 149
  and multiple currency
    reserves   148, 149
  and private wealth holders
    141
  and redundancy problem
    142
  reform proposals of   83, 84,
    147–50
  reserve composition under
    134, 135, 136
  reserve supply in long run
    148–50
  and restrictions on trade   80
  and Rio de Janeiro
    Agreements   150
  and Roosa bonds   147
  rules of the game   129, 146
  and seigniorage problem
    143, 144
  shortcomings of   131–47
  theoretical blueprint of
    128–31
  and United Kingdom   137
  and United States   135, 136
  and World Bankers   128–31
Gold guarantees   147, 149
Goldsmiths
  liquidity ratio   160
  and social seigniorage
    distribution   159–62
Gold specie standard   97
Gold standard
  and adjustment mechanism
    91–4, 177
  and Bank of England   102

classical model of   89–94
and discount rates   100
and foreign currency
   holdings   131, 132
and freedom   105
and government interven-
   tion   93, 94, 99, 105
history of   21, 101–6, 109,
   118
insurance features of   93
and internationalism   119
and income adjustments
   95, 96
and mercantilism   104
and monetary policy   99,
   100
and multiple money supply
   expansion   98
and nationalism   104
and price stability   92
and purchasing power
   maintenance   173, 174
and quantity theory of
   money   89–91
and real world modifications
   of theory   94–101
reform proposals for   82, 83
and resource flows   92, 93
and short-term capital
   flows   94, 95
and United Kingdom   100,
   101
Goldstein, H.   190
Gold tranche   137, 181
Graham, F.   190
Gresham's law   102
Grimm, B.   15
Group of Ten   55, 84
Grubel, H. G.   39n, 57n,
   59n, 188, 190

Harrod, R.   79n, 165, 187,
190
Hart, A. G.   158, 159, 187,
   190
Harvard University   94
Heilperin, M.   82, 189
Heller, H.   188
Heller, W.   79n
Hinshaw, R. H.   188
Hirschman, A. O.   158, 159,
   190
Horie, J.   190
Hume, D.   90, 188

Income elasticity
   of demand for reserves   66,
   72
Income adjustments
   and demand for reserves
   45–50
   and gold standard   95, 96
India   103
Inflation tax   66, 174
Ingram, J.   83, 188
Integration
   and demand for reserves   54
Intellectuals
   and monetary reform   75,
   76
Interest arbitrage   57–60
Interest charges
   and centrally created
      reserves   159–62
   and demand for reserves
      62–4
   and developing countries
      166
   under I.M.F.   180
   and Roosa plan   164
   and social seigniorage
      distribution   159–62
Interest equalization tax
   25, 51

International co-operation
and demand for reserves
53–6
and speculative capital
flows 60
International central bank
see Supra-national bank
International Monetary
Fund
credit with 30
founding of 163, 164
and interest charges 180
lending policies of 179
par values under 169
and quotas 170, 183
reform of 83, 84, 149, 150,
164
reserves provided by
134–7
and Rio de Janeiro
Agreements 150, 183–5
and scarce currency clause
180, 181
International money
see International reserves
International monetary
organization
adequacy tests of 75–81
and foreign aid 25
history of 21–3
and payments imbalances
23
and tariff policy 25, 26
and World Bankers 24
International monetary
reform
and central bankers 75, 76
and changes in technology
22
and intellectuals 75, 76
and politics 20
and world welfare 20

International monetary
reform proposals surveyed
flexible exchange rates 81,
82
gold standard 82, 83
improved capital markets
83
gold exchange standard 83,
84
supra-national bank 84,
85
International reserves
and adjustment mechanism
45–50
and attitudes toward risk
73
and borrowing facilities
180
and capital balance
instabilities 56–62, 72
composition of 132–7
and co-operation 53–6
and exchange guarantees
175
and exchange rate flexibility
31–4
and forced lending 180
gold, as 136
under gold exchange
standard 128–31, 143
and I.M.F. positions 136
income elasticity of demand
for 66, 72
and income levels 68
inflation tax on 174
interdependence of demand
for 70
and interest charges $42n$,
62–5
and integration 54
liquidity yield of 63–5
and marginal propensity to

import 70–71
measurement of 74
and national currencies 21,
22, 30, 136
nature of 19, 28–31
opportunity cost of 42n
and price changes 66, 67
and purchasing power
maintenance 173–5
and Rio de Janeiro
Agreements 183–5
shortage of 80
and short-term capital
flows 56–62
and trade levels 71, 74
and trade stability 71, 72
and uncertainty 43, 64
and value guarantees 174
International short-term
capital flows
see Short-term capital flows
Internationalism
and gold standard 119
Italy
balance-of-payment
problems 23
credit arrangements 60
and gold standard 102
Group of Ten member 60

Jacobson, P. 147, 190
Japan
and gold standard 103
Group of Ten member 55
and optimum currency
area 123
quotas of 165
Johnson, H G. 15, 187, 190

Kaldor, N. 158, 159, 190
Kenen, P. 164, 168–70,
187–190

Keynes, J. M. 84, 163, 165,
169, 170, 178–80, 190
Keynes Plan
see Keynes, J. M.
Keynesian economics 31,
46–8, 58, 96, 158
Kindleberger, C. P. 35n,
36n, 187, 188
Kramer, R. 187

Lary, H. 189
League of Nations 55
Lerner, A. P. 189
Liquidity
of goldsmiths 160
of World Bankers 138–40
see also International
reserves
London 95
Lutz, F. 147, 190
Luxemburg 121

Machlup, F. 97n, 187, 188
Marginal propensity to
import 47, 70, 71, 96
Marshall-Lerner condition
35n, 46
Marshall Plan 55
Marshallian offer curve 36n
Mayer, H. 15
McKinnon, R. 122, 189
Meade, J. 35n, 36n, 81,
187–9
Mercantilism 90, 91, 104
Mertens, J. E. 189
Modigliani, F. 164, 168–70,
190
Money
characteristics of 29
history of evolution 29
national *v.* international
153

role of 19
see also International
    reserves
Multiple currency reserve
    proposal 148, 149
Mundell, R. A. 121, 187–90
Murphy, C. 189

National sovereignty
  and supra-national bank
    152, 153
Nationalism
  and flexible exchange rates
    119, 120
  and gold standard 104
  during 1930s 104
  and seigniorage distribution
    158
Neo-classical synthesis 66
Netherlands 23, 55, 146
New York Federal Reserve
    Bank 145, 173*n*
New Zealand 123
Norway 131
Nurkse, R. 131, 188–90

Operation Twist 59, 61
Optimum currency areas
  and currency value 122
  and employment stability
    122
  and factor mobility 122
  and speculators 118, 122
  and thin markets 118, 122
Organization for Economic
    Co-operation and
    Development 55
Pfister, R. L. 188, 189
Phelps, E. 47*n*
Philippines 123
Phillips curve 47
  diagram 48, 69

Posthuma, S. 147, 190
Pound sterling
  see Sterling
Price elasticities
  see Elasticities of price
Prices
  and demand for reserves
    65–9
  and gold standard 92
  stability and unemployment
    trade-off 47, 48, 69

Quantity theory of money
    89–91
Quotas
  and adjustment mechanism
    179
  determination at Bretton
    Woods 165
  under I.M.F. 164
  under Rio de Janeiro
    Agreements 167, 183

Random walk 39–42, 73
Real balance effect 65
Redundancy problem 142
Reserves
  see International reserves
Rhomberg, R. 189
Rio de Janeiro Agreements of
    1967
  and adjustment mechanism
    181, 182, 184
  and gold exchange standard
    150
  and gold guarantee 174,
    184
  and gold holdings 171, 184
  and quantity of reserves
    created 167, 182, 183,
    185
  and quotas 165, 180

and seigniorage distribution
164, 165, 183
voting procedures under
184
Risk and demand for
reserves 73
Roosa, R. 83, 84, 147, 164,
166, 167, 190
Roosa bonds 147
Root, F. 187
Rothwell, K. J. 188, 189
Rueff, J. 82, 189
Rules of the game
and adjustment mechanism
177
under gold exchange
standard 129, 146
and supra-national bank
177
Russia 102, 103, 105, 131

Scammel, W. M. 187
Scarce currency clause 180,
181
Second World War 49, 51,
55, 60, 78, 105, 125, 128,
134, 135, 137, 163, 164,
169, 178
Seigniorage
and income redistribution
145
nature of 143–5
present value of 143–4
U.K. and U.S. benefits from
144
see also Social seigniorage
Short-term capital flows
and demand for reserves
56–62
under gold standard 94,
95
and welfare 61

Silver money 29, 102
Smith, A. 19, 107, 108
Social seigniorage
central government method
of distribution 156–9
and developing countries
157
free market method of
distribution 159–62
and goldsmiths 159–61
and interest payments
159–62
and Keynes-White plans
163
measurement of 154–6
and nationalism 158
present value of 155
and Stamp plan 157
transactions demand method
of distribution 162–6
United States, value in 156
and world public goods
157
see also Seigniorage
Sohmen, E. 189
South African gold fields
103
Soviet Union
see Russia
South America 22, 123
Special Drawing Rights 164,
165, 171, 183–5
see also Rio de Janeiro
Agreements
Speculation
Canadian experience 118
and capital flows 60
destabilizing 39, 62, 116
and flexible exchange rates
116–18
and floating population of
losers 117

and gold exchange standard
141
and optimum currency
areas 118
stabilizing 62, 117
during U.S. Civil War 118
Spraos, J. 15
Stamp, M. 84, 157, 162,
167, 190
Sterling
devaluation effects on 49,
50
as reserves 21, 30, 133–7,
164
and shifts into gold 65
Stoll, H. 39n, 188
Supra-national bank
and adjustment mechanism
175–83
and commodity backing for
obligations 158
and gold 168–73
and interest payments
160–62
and national monetary
history 151, 152
and national sovereignty
152–3
nature of obligations issued
153
and private means of
payment 153
and quantity of reserves
created 166–8
and quotas 164–6
reform proposals survey
84, 85
Rio de Janeiro Agreements
183–5
and social seigniorage
distribution 154–66
and value maintenance of
obligations issued
173–5
Sweden 55, 131
Switzerland 55, 102

Tariffs 25, 45, 50–52, 135
Taussig, F. 94, 95, 97
Telser, L. 189
Tew, B. 187
Tinbergen, J. 158, 159,
190
Tobin, J. 190
Triffin, R. 15, 84, 101, 137,
147, 161, 167–9, 171, 180
181, 187, 190
Triffin Plan
see Triffin, R.
Tsiang, S. C. 189

Uncertainty
and demand for reserves
39, 40, 64
Underdeveloped countries
see Developing countries
Unemployment 47–9
United Kingdom
and credit arrangement 60
deficits 23, 51, 65, 79, 133
devaluation 24, 49, 50
and foreign aid 25
under gold standard 95,
100–102
Group of Ten 55
and I.M.F. 163, 165
and surcharges on imports
51
and tariffs 26
as World Banker 21–4,
138–40, 144, 145
United States
and credit arrangements 60
deficits 23, 51, 65

devaluation 24
direct controls 25, 51
economic growth 105
and flexible exchange rates
   118, 121
and foreign aid 25
and full employment 79n
and gold sales 170, 172
under gold standard 102
Group of Ten 55
and I.M.F. 163, 165
and Operation Twist 59
and redundancy problem
   142
and seigniorage 138–40,
   156
and tariffs 26
as World Banker 21–4,
   135, 138–40, 144, 145

Vickers, D. 15

Wallich, H. 83, 147, 190
Ward, R. 187
Washington Agreements of
   1968 172, 183, 184

West Germany
   see Germany
West Virginia 121
White, H. 163, 165, 190
Whittlesey, R. 15
World Banker
   and confidence crisis 137,
      138
   and deficits 26, 34, 142
   and devaluation 142
   and gold exchange standard
      128–30
   liquidity ratio of 130, 138
   U.K. as 137–40
   U.S. as 136–40
World central bank
   see Supra-national bank
World monetary reform
   see International monetary
      reform

Yap 29
Yeager, L. 187–9
Yudin, L. 188

Zolotas 83, 147, 190